STAGE FOUR,
FIVE ALARM

Warning: this book contains the words God and Jesus
and is full of faith, hope, and love.

JIM BALANESI

Inspiring Voices®
A Service of Guideposts

Inspiring Voices books may be ordered through booksellers or by contacting:

Inspiring Voices
1663 Liberty Drive
Bloomington, IN 47403
www.inspiringvoices.com
1-(866) 697-5313

ISBN: 978-1-4624-0198-7 (sc)
ISBN: 978-1-4624-0199-4 (e)

Library of Congress Control Number: 2012941888

Printed in the United States of America

Inspiring Voices rev. date: 06/18/2012

Table of Contents

To my dear wife

I have proudly and lovingly dedicated this book to my holy Father, with all of my love and gratitude for saving me and thereby giving me another chance at living a holy life—and to my wife, Cindy. She was tirelessly there for me with her super-supportive attitude and innate care-giving skills throughout all of my trials and tribulations—even as she coped with a number of situations in her own personal life that would have broken most spirits. Maybe someday she'll be able to share two particular stories that show again and again God's miraculous grace, love, and awesome healing powers. Ours is a living God, here and now, today, tomorrow, and forever. Thank you, my Sweaty-Pie, for truly saving and enriching my life by listening to God so that I now have Him and His Son, Jesus, as my employers! ("Sweaty" is a clean nickname, originally just a misspelled word, which is a whole other story in itself.)

Preface

This book is not about whining and woe-is-me attitudes. It is a chronicle of events: my journey over the last five +years, from the place where my wife and I began, to a new spiritual way of life today. A series of life-threatening, life-changing events and our actively keeping God in our daily lives turned everything around.

We're hoping that this book will act as an encouragement and inspiration to others. When you feel like crying out, "Why me?" or "Why us, God?," we want to help you turn that feeling around and prevent it from becoming a mind-set so negative that you become stuck in whatever situation you're facing.

Instead, wonder what God has in store for you; expect that something good is going to come out of this or that, and take another approach. Have a strong faith in God, and don't stop there. Remember this Scripture: "With God all things are possible." Luke 18:27

This book will show you how God miraculously—and I mean *miraculously*—got us through to where we are now living in daily peace, abundance, love, and gratitude. I don't think an hour passes on any day without the thought of *Praise God!* coming from our hearts. It's become a new life, a great life to live in His peace. I'm not talking about that drug-induced, mind-altered hippie peace from the sixties. This is all about having God's true peace inside our souls. And what a joy it is! We'll help you get there too by sharing our stories.

Cindy and I are just regular people. Of the two of us, she was much more into living a Christian lifestyle and always trying to practice what she was learning by following that path. I, on the other hand, can't say that I played that role or any role very well, but I'm an okay guy. I'm five years her senior, and we have both now sailed well into our fifties.

I have personally looked back and felt that I wasted most of that time for one big reason: I didn't actively have God in my life, nor did I use the Bible as my life's guide. "I could've (would have) been a contender," as the famous saying goes, if I had. However, I now see where *everything* in my life has meaning, and it's all come full circle to where I am today. I see why I did this, tried that, left this and that, and received—or took—different opportunities along the way, but nothing lasted. And so I came to my recent realization of why I'm here today, living with all of this gratitude and love for God. It's a puzzle I've now pieced together, so I can clearly see the picture. Therefore, I'm not kicking myself or trying to go back and be a "contender." Instead, I believe that God already knew the whole story, and that's where I now put all of my faith and trust today—in Him and His Son. You can too!

Cindy and I hope that you'll receive something from our saga. We've prayed that you will get something worthwhile for the time you've invested in reading this book. We realize that, despite all the stuff Cindy and I experienced, it could have and might have been *so much worse*!

When you go through adversities and tragedies, as we all do, catch yourself and realize that it could have been so much worse than it actually is or was. Then give thanks that it wasn't worse, and give the situation to the right source: our living God and His Son, Jesus.

We've all had situations—car accidents, falls, fires, loss—where the outcomes could have been so much worse. Our own situations are often nothing compared to what so many others have gone through. I recently saw video clips of returning war veterans with missing limbs. Those heroes have had it so much worse than I have—so much worse. God, please bless all of our soldiers.

We've all experienced terrible situations in our own lives, first hand. We don't want to think about most worst-case scenarios, but maybe we should so we can *really* give thanks where it's due. What if this or that had happened? Just watch today's popular cable TV show *I Survived*, and you'll see how some terrible situations actually turned out. It could've been so much worse in each one of those stories.

Thank you for giving this book a try, and may God bless you and yours!

Acknowledgments

I must say that I was very blessed and privileged to have had so many family members, friends, and customers—from the picture framing industry, the café, and my early years—who kindly sent cards and e-mails and made phone calls to let me know of their prayers and thoughts of me. I am still so grateful for their love and kindness over the many years. I tried sending periodic updates to keep many of them posted on what was happening to me. Writing this little book should update all of those who still may be interested. Thank you for your love, care, and desire to keep me in your thoughts.

It was pretty cool when Cindy had that gift shop up at the lake. It was a Christian Book & Gift Store with so much great material. You've read by now—at least I hope you have—that God determined your outcome back before you were even born. Here are just a few of the resources available to you: "If God be for us, who can be against us" (Romans 8:31). "No weapon formed against you shall prosper," (Isaiah 54:17). "With God, all things are possible."

Your faith, trust, and belief in God must be very strong for any of this to work. It's not easy to turn over your life to God or to His Son, Jesus Christ. It's not easy, until you see and experience it with your own mind and eyes. We have to stay in this state, constantly growing, until the Holy Spirit is actively living inside of us every moment. Let Him in, and surrender the rest of the clutter in your life. Ask for forgiveness for your sins. Acknowledge that Jesus died for your sins on the cross, rose from the dead, and sits at the right hand of God, His Father. He promises that you will prosper and that He will always be with you.

Isn't this better than keeping up some false barricade and believing that you are better, stronger, and more qualified than someone we can't see, touch, or hear but whose works we experience all around us? We can see the beauty and learn of the miraculous stories and feel the joy of peace. Just be quiet and listen. He will talk to you. Talk to Him and then sit quietly.

The Resource section at the end of this book is only a partial list of excellent shows, ministries, and pastors who are filling our daily lives with the best spiritual food. There's always something good to watch on TV, and the ministers and pastors will become your favorite talents, as they have become for us. You'll feel invigorated and full of hope as you fight the fight alongside God, your commander in chief.

I just received an envelope in the mail from a friend we met through the Christian Gift Shop that Cindy opened after the fire. This particular husband and wife became special to us over the short time that Cindy had the store. She had told me about them and that the husband, Bob, had gone through lung cancer as well—and that he didn't even smoke. Cindy encouraged me to meet him, and I finally got the chance. He was such a sweet man, and so is his wife, Debbie. We would meet often for coffee and tea and share our lives touched by cancer. Unfortunately, Bob had to leave his wife of many, many years when he was called to heaven. I can see him in my mind as clearly as if he had just walked into my garage. He had a smile and a twinkle in his eyes that would bring such warmth to my heart. His departure left his beautiful wife alone, but she knows that someday they'll be reunited for eternity.

Bob's passing was several years ago, and to this day, Debbie and I still correspond almost daily via e-mail. When I came downstairs after a short nap, Cindy handed me an envelope sent by Debbie. It contained a thoughtful card and a very generous check with instructions for us to put the check toward publishing this book that you're now holding. I was shocked but very grateful to have received this extremely generous gift. I called Debbie immediately. Earlier, I had read one of my daily e-mails from Joel and Victoria Osteen, "Today's Word," with a message entitled, "Fulfilling the Law of Christ." It talked about an act of kindness and generosity, demonstrated by what Debbie had just shared. In this case, "lightening someone's burden" meant that we received that generous check in order to help us publish this book.

How did Debbie know that she would be removing a financial burden from us? God knew, and we believe God directed her. You will see His love everywhere if you just look. And remember this: "coincidence is when God chooses to remain anonymous."

CHAPTER 1

It Could've Been Worse, So Much Worse

This is a true story of how my wife and I overcame cancer and a fire. These experiences took us on a new journey, getting to know what our lives are truly all about. Since we first married, the Devil has tried to break us apart with each hardship that came our way.

Instead of giving up, we followed God and His Word, which made us stronger with each step, even though most times we were struggling to move forward. We had the desire to win these battles, as hard as they were, and God gave us the courage and guidance, strength and knowledge, to continue on together. Our characters and our spirits could have been blown apart by these tragedies I'm about to share—if not for our growing relationship with God and His Son, Jesus. Their love has kept us together and made us into the strong individuals that we are today. Our appreciation for what only God could have done is renewed daily and can never be forgotten or taken for granted.

If you're one who still needs proof of God or His Son, Jesus, then you've opened the right book. Don't call any of this a coincidence. A "coincidence is when God chooses to remain anonymous." Things don't just happen. Whether it is by the will of God or our own free will—which He already knows about—everything happens for a reason. I'd rather be on the side of God's will. I've been on the other side for most of my life, and I moved over here because of God's love for me in providing me another chance at living life as He wanted me to live.

I may have lost many of you at this point, but please stay with me, as it will all come together. Who knew that I'd ever be where I am right now, writing a book about my redemption and appreciation? God has always known and seen something good in me, as He does in you. I am just now realizing it.

Smoking for Thirty-Nine-Plus Years, and What Did It Get Me?

What causes half a million people to die each year, is legal to buy, and is as—or more—addictive than heroin? You've got it; and I let it get me as early as fourteen years of age. I followed the leader because I too wanted to be cool; then I became stupid, and then I couldn't stop. I was a follower and not a good one at that. In the beginning of my habit, most cigarettes came from snitching them from a family member or a friend's parents. Every once in a while, I'd score my own pack from a seedy merchant or friend of a friend.

I spent years and years puffing about 421,200 butts, and my Dad would say, "You're sucking in the smoke down to your toenails." I was so hooked, I was like an addict. I consumed a pack to two packs (and sometimes more) every day for about forty years. That approximately calculates out to a whopping $59,427 dollars, literally up in smoke, figured on a rising scale beginning at around fifty-five cents a pack to the $4.50 price seven years ago.

An enormous amount of stupidity, a waste of energy, and financial instability resulted from all of those purchases. For kids or adults to start smoking now, it is just a sick and ridiculous act—an act of suicide, when you come right down to it. There's so much anti-smoking material available and out in the public today, more so than ever before. Smoking is a total waste of money and resources, and it's a means of destruction to the body that God has blessed us with.

You have to accept responsibility for your decision to take up smoking. No one is forcing you or bullying you today. I remember when we had this club at the rear of a neighborhood grocery store. The main initiation was to smoke a cigarette. Yes, they were the red-boxed Marlboro. The days of being barraged with pro-smoking ads and television commercials are over, at least here in the United States. Smoking is almost totally prohibited from all restaurants, bars, and other public environments.

Contrary to what we ignorantly believed, smoking doesn't lead just to lung cancer. That small, cancerous cell can metastasize itself to all parts of your body. It got into my shoulder, vertebrae, and brain. Smoking can often lead to death, stroke, high blood pressure, seizures, and on and on. I'll be sharing some of those areas with you too.

Where do all of those butts go, anyway? Many smokers, myself included, think that disposing of the butt on the ground, in a flower pot, or just out the window is okay, legal, and our right. We'd do it right smack in front of others' homes, yards, and property—which is no better than leaving your shopping cart wherever you want, or littering, or spitting chewing gum out in the parking lot. Who's watching us, anyway?

I was. I sat in my truck, bored, as Cindy started our grocery shopping in the veggie and fruit departments. I watched a person return to his car, look around for a moment, and then leave his cart by the next car over. I saw one huge guy drop his litter at a gas station. His body was partially hidden by the tank. Big, tough me says, "Hey, you dropped something!" He knew he had and came around the pump. After seeing just how big he was, I quickly said, "I'll get it, sir. Sorry."

There was a time when our moms and dads puffed away in the car or in our homes. My dad and his friends did, and their children followed their example. I can still hear my dad puffing away as he gave me haircuts out in the garage, while my friends were outside playing. I can still hear him suck in and blow out as he held the cigarette in his lips and squinted through the smoke, trying to cut my hair. Ashes would often fall along with my hair onto my lap. He honestly didn't inhale. I don't hold my dad responsible for possibly getting me hooked or ultimately sick from secondhand smoke. It wasn't an issue back then, and it only became one in recent history. Thank God that it became a *huge* issue!

I can't believe how many times I smoked in bed, in the bathroom, kitchen, restaurant, office, or while grocery shopping. For some crazy reason, I can still visualize one particular butt container at the end of an aisle at a Safeway Store from many years ago. Smoking was very convenient back then. We could light up while on an airplane, at the movies, and even in a hospital. Thank God that all of this insanity is coming to an end, at least in most places here in the United States.

One time when I was a senior in high school, I went to have a smoke in the head. Kids were coming and going, when all of a sudden I was staring at our principal through the smoke-filled restroom. He took down my name and told me to go see the Dean of Boys immediately. Before long, I was sitting in his office. I told the dean that I was so sorry and that I was going to be dead meat when I got home and that my spring break would be nothing but torture. It happened to be the Friday before our week-long vacation began.

After a moment or two of consideration, the Dean said, "Okay, Balanesi, you're a pretty good kid. I'll pretend to catch you when you return from the break." He went on to say that he'd notify my parents and begin my three-day suspension then. I was so grateful—to him, not God. I thanked him and went on my way. Thinking back, he was like a tough, old Marine Gunnery Sergeant in a suit. He had the hair, the mean look, and everything.

I immediately went straight home after school and told my mom, because my guilt was getting the best of me. I pleaded with her not to tell my dad, and she mercifully agreed for my sake. I was stuck at home for the entire day during the three-day suspension and could only leave the house after school let out.

Ten years later, after the military and while in college, the entire event came back to mind. I was starting my last semester of student teaching at another high school across town from the one where I'd barely graduated. In college, I had buckled down. My major was Art Education, and I graduated with a BA with Distinction.

The night before my student teaching assignment was to begin, I had to find the school I was to report to. I had never been to that high school because of its tough reputation, even though it was in the same city I'd grown up in and referred to as my home town. I had seen a few of the tough guys there, and they were scary. I had always thought I was somewhat of a tough guy (behind certain friends), but I learned, especially in the Marines, that there are *so* many tougher than I am. Maybe my toughness came years later with the fight of my life.

I arrived on time that morning and soon located my resident teachers that I had been assigned to. I quickly learned, after being on the campus for only a short time, that there was a designated smoking area for the students. I thought, *Wow*. I'd been one of the many "cool" guys who had been caught and punished so that one day these kids could legally smoke on campus without being suspended.

I was shown the teachers' lounge and noticed none other than the principal who had caught me in the restroom ten years earlier. Only now he was the vice principal of this high school. I never brought up that old incident with him and went on with my daily assignments. I don't think that he ever recognized me anyway. At least I could have a smoke in the lounge with all of the other teachers.

This is not a "Stop Smoking" book. I just wanted to go back in order to move forward. I'm laying out a situation that happened in my life, something that has led me to be with you now. I can't go back and change any of it, nor can you, but I can use what I've learned and experienced to share this story. Understanding how it all comes together calms my spirit and makes sense out of all the stuff that happened then and is happening now. Please believe me: I once beat myself up over the money wasted, the lives I've hurt, where I went wrong, and so on. Today, right now, I've learned to accept all of this stuff as part of the building process for acquiring wisdom in my life and learning to appreciate what is here and yet to come. It's all happened for a reason unknown to us. God knows, though! He knows everything.

Well, you could bet your bank on what I was doing, even on the day my dear dad took his last breath. I was smoking. And I smoked another part of that same year until I tried quitting once again. My dad had smoked most of his life, as did his dad, before succumbing to the terrors of emphysema and finally taking his last breath.

As I mentioned previously, my dad didn't inhale in the traditional way. Instead, he just puffed and blew and surrounded himself in smoky clouds carrying the liquid poisons that would seep down his throat. Like our mom said, "He *reeked* of smoke." He smoked a pipe, now and then, and many cigars as well, for years. A good amount of smoke made it into his lungs from simply breathing, so he actually was inhaling in an alternative way that ultimately gave him lung cancer at seventy-seven.

One afternoon, he fell off a ladder while puttering out in his garage. That fall landed him a trip to the emergency room, which gave him a wake-up call, telling him that he was loaded with cancer in his lungs and his days were numbered. He got himself ready in his mind. He started saying that he'd had a good life with just one regret. He felt as though he hadn't taken enough time to read to his three sons.

But he had taught us how to fish, and we'd camped at many lakes. Most importantly, he'd led us by always setting a good example. We never heard our parents fight. We never—even though we lived off the single income of a telephone company employee's paycheck—never went without anything. For me that included private classical guitar and karate lessons. Our home was a very secure and safe place, but one where you would never have a party. Our mom and dad were strict and tough, especially our dad.

After receiving radiation treatments in the area of his lung, my dad was pretty well in agreement with his doctors that his time would be short and he should get his life in order. He had no desire for chemotherapy, which was an option to prolong his time a bit. He felt that he'd had a good life and that he would deal with his situation in the comfort of his own home with my mom by his side. My folks had been married a little over fifty-eight years and had lived in the same home for most of them. Those super-special people of hospice came in and assisted my mom in caring for my dad during his last days. He quickly became bedridden, made of skin and bones, and he looked like an old, white-haired, bearded man who was dying. However, through all of these changes, he was still my dad and a giant in my mind.

Cindy and I had been able to give him a new Cadillac just before he fell off that ladder. We were doing quite well, and Cindy was so unselfish to help me fulfill a dream. We'll always remember the look on his face the evening that Cindy drove it into his driveway with a huge white bow on the hood. He was sitting at his work bench, smoking a cigar. As always, his garage door was the only one open, day and night, most of each and every day for many, many years.

It was only because of my wife's true generosity and love that we were able to pull this off. Unfortunately, my dad was only able to drive his new car for a short time, but it gave him such enjoyment driving to and from his radiation treatments over in Palo Alto. Shortly after that, his driving days were over. The Caddy sat out in his garage until he passed away.

What a great feeling it was to fulfill a dream I'd had for so many years: to present my dad with a new Cadillac. Thanks to God and to my wife, I was able to see that day and the expression of shock and joy on his face. I was so blessed to have him as my dad. The thought brings me back to an evening when I was in elementary school, when we had a father-and-son night in the auditorium. We sang the song that Paul Peterson once sang on the *Donna Reed Show*: "My Dad." That really puts a knot in my throat! I'll be back . . .

Cindy had lived through the passing of her own mother from the deadly hazards of smoking—specifically emphysema. Unfortunately, I had never met her before she passed on at the early age of fifty-two. Her death was the result of smoking, and she became another casualty to be added to the many lives that this nasty, deadly habit takes. But did that stop us from smoking? Hell, no, of course not! We were snagged—hook, line, and sinker. Sadly, I never had the pleasure of meeting Cindy's mom, for she died a year before fate put Cindy and me together. I'm told that Cindy's mom and I would have been the best of friends, and I feel that in my heart. To this day, I see the pain that her early passing left on her family.

And there you have it. In our small family alone, cigarettes caused the deaths of my dad, my granddad, and Cindy's mother—and they were still messing with me. I thought, *You're not getting me or any other family members, Big Tobacco companies. How can you make your living off killing people? I'm still not done getting shots in for what you do!*

Can you imagine having a job selling such a product? This is our free will working at its best. Come on, now. Does it take having lung cancer to understand the problem? Apparently so, when one doesn't have a strong relationship with our Father and His Son. In order to solidify this conclusion for myself, I had to return "to the valley of the shadow of death" (Psalm 23).

It is now the beginning of January 2011. I had been living under the assumption—which was all I wanted to know—that I was still in complete remission, based on the findings after a visit to the doctor last year. A "complete" report said more, since other doctors wrote me off and saw only doom and gloom for the rest of my short life. Thank God that I didn't buy into their assumptions. Shame on them! Actually, I want to take that last line back, since their negative predictions inadvertently gave me the fuel needed to ignite my will to live.

Just recently, from the monthly testing that my anointed oncologist continues to do on me, Cindy and I learned that it showed little irregularities in my brain. Further testing and a dreaded MRI had confirmed that it is not scar tissue from a previous bout with brain cancer but a small reoccurrence of brain cancer that has metastasized again. Even as I write this sentence, I'm in full faith that God has already cleaned up that little cancerous glitch. I don't feel a thing. I have no discomfort, headaches, or other abnormalities that may arise from this kind of reoccurrence.

I'm comparing this current situation to the original condition in my brain found a couple of years ago. That time was different, because I did feel irregularities in my body telling me that something wasn't good, and I felt a pressure in the back of my head.

Sometimes I saw a colorful kaleidoscope appear, moving around the edge of our TV. It appeared around my car headlights as I began an early morning trip down the hill from our little lake house to the major freeway. My wife and her sister were following right behind me, watching my every move on the road. We were going to an appointment to see my oncologist, who wanted to see me. It was stupid to drive, and I knew it, but I didn't want them to know any more about my condition, since they had originally ratted me out to my nurse, and I was most certainly going in for another dreaded MRI. My oncologist had already prepared for my arrival at the clinic and ultimately a stay in the hospital right up the street.

Not only had I begun to see the colorful activity around the TV screen, but Cindy was getting her new Christian Gift Store ready to open. I was spending much of my time helping out. It just so happened that I kept feeling some kind of pressure behind my head. It was annoying, but it was not disabling me. I had been wearing my headpiece for my cell phone everywhere, and I thought that might have something to do with the feeling. A combination of this and that led me to believe that this most recent reoccurrence was not showing itself as it had in the past.

There were two other things that happened. I had my laptop at that home, so we could always keep abreast of our accounts. I went online, but I could not remember my account password. I had not even a hint as to what it might be. After I called and cleared that up, I looked at an entry for a local eatery where Cindy and I ate dinner sometimes and noticed that it looked like I had entered, *Greatest job ever, Larry!* and a whopping four-hundred-dollar tip. Of course I immediately called the owner and got him all shook-up. So the rat finks knew something was up, and I kind of did too. I didn't want to know any of the details or the prognosis, though. Here I was, going back into battle again. Cindy had done an excellent job of coordinating family members that would be able to stay with me and drive me back and forth to my treatments. She needed to get back to her new store, as she would be opening it soon.

It is truly thanks to God that I am able to be here and dedicate this book to my wife. I'm able to write this because of His grace and her true love and dedication to our marriage all along the way. We have both tripped and fallen so many times, but God has helped us up, and we have stayed by His side—especially now that I am finally getting it. The old adage that "things can always be worse" is as true for us today as it has been for millions of people in the past and will be in the future. We have been so blessed by God and His Son Jesus—as you are about to read.

Back before we met, Cindy was over in Vallejo, praying to meet someone like me and even asking that he have an Italian heritage. She was going through a divorce from her first husband and was raising their two sons virtually alone.

Meanwhile, I was up in Windsor, California, sitting outside on the porch, smoking a cigarette and wondering where the "right one" was as well. I was looking across the landscape toward Vallejo, trying to find her in my mind. I was going through my second separation, getting the boot, and would be moving to Vallejo soon, as part of an agreement that I would take over a condo that we shared with another couple. I referred to it as the "commuter condo," since it was used by the wives in order to work at that location, which would've been a long daily drive for them. This condo would keep me close to my son, who was going to a preschool close to his mom's new assignment. My son was going on four at that time. I had to be close to him, because I wanted to be with him at least half the time.

When Cindy and I did meet and I was invited over for dinner, we discovered that she had been washing a few dishes and looking out the window, facing toward the exact location where I'd been having a cigarette that night. I had been looking toward Vallejo and seeing her at that same window. It was so incredible! Boy, was this a match made by divine design?

I believe that this still happens today. Cindy and I actually met through a business club that I joined and met weekly for breakfast. The club had to change restaurants for a few weeks while the original place was having new carpets installed. I walked into the substitute restaurant for the first time, took one look at Cindy, and fell in love.

I was just what she had been praying for too. We were meant to be together, but it had taken a while—about twenty years. As the saying goes: "in God's time." Both our families were Italian and were meant to be part of the bigger picture. We were just a few years behind/

What Did Smoking Have to Do with Me? Everything!

When I had quit smoking in the past—for a day, a couple of days, or a week or two—my breathing had returned quickly to where I could definitely feel the difference. Having to climb stairs to see customers in San Francisco was not a problem after a short time without cigarettes.

I remember calling on one particular customer on the third floor. Shortly after quitting, I'd zip up those stairs. I tried using many of the quit-smoking remedies, including the patch, gum, acupuncture, self-help books, and cold turkey—all to no avail over many, many attempts. The chewing gum with nicotine was the only product that seemed to help me, and ultimately it helped me quit for well over five years now. Who do you think I thank for that? Yes, thank you, God.

When I was able to quit for a longer period of time, it was the chewing gum that worked best to beat most of my urges to smoke. The good part was, I smelled better. My customers were no longer able to smell my arrival. Now I know just how nasty is the smell of a smoker. Before you quit, everything smells fine. You figure that people are just exaggerating about the offensive odor on your clothes and body. Now I know how awful I smelled, even after spraying fu-fu on me and chewing a fresh piece of gum before each visit.

I recovered and enjoyed the good feeling inside. Why would I ever want to start smoking again? As an addict, the negatives had almost always overpowered the pluses of being smoke-free!

I went to Las Vegas for a yearly trade show, and going to and from the airports and being on the plane was not a problem. I had my nicotine-enhanced chewing gum with me and was feeling good. I didn't have to look for excuses to leave our booth for a lousy cigarette break. It was so nice and comforting to finally have some control, even though I had to rely on the gum.

Remember my saying that I would look for excuses or something to happen that made it okay to light up a cigarette? Unfortunately, I immediately went back to smoking upon my arrival home from the trade show. It had been one of my longest spells without smoking ever. But heck, I had a pretty good excuse, so I was back at it and so was Cindy. That made it okay in my eyes, and the idiotic behavior continued.

Another year passed with me smoking my life away and enjoying my mornings having coffee and chitchat with my wife before we each started our work day. I'd smoke at least ten cigarettes before leaving to go see my customers. Over time, Cindy began to hear my breathing. I had started feeling a bit sluggish, and my breathing was not as clear as when I had smoked before. My dad had always told my brother and me about hearing "that little voice within," referring to the wheezing sound you hear when your lungs are congested, especially when it's quiet and you're lying down. I happened to run into my aunt and uncle while I was out calling on my accounts one day up north. When my uncle asked about his brother, he mentioned that the Achilles' heel in our family was our chests, our breathing. I never forgot what he said. I even told my younger brother what our uncle had said regarding our bodies.

Cindy insisted that what she heard coming from my throat or lungs had nothing to do with the new allergy I thought I had, and she wanted me to go see my primary care doctor *immediately*. I fought her all the way. When I went to see him, he agreed with my assumption that I was merely congested, and he prescribed some nasal spray for allergies. That didn't seem to change what Cindy was hearing, and I continued to disagree with her wishes for me to go back to the doctor for more tests. I told you early on that I was an idiot—a good guy, from what I've been told, but a stubborn idiot! Eventually, I became worried as well.

It was January of 2006 when a large, puffy protrusion appeared on top of my left shoulder. It began to bother me, and after a good while I went back to my doctor, who said that it could be bursitis. He gave me a cortisone shot on top of my shoulder. The pain persisted, meaning that the shot didn't work at all, and the protrusion remained. Along my sales route, I would ask customers about it when they asked how I was doing. I'd eagerly tell them about that bubble on my shoulder, hoping for, "That's nothing. I had something like that. It'll go away." One customer said that he'd had something like that, and it was maybe a "ganglion cyst." The doctor had treated his, and it was fine now. I was hoping for the same kind of thing in my case.

Now we were into the spring bass fishing season, and nothing was going to stop me from going out. I was still smoking, hearing that little voice, and carrying-on with that puffy shoulder protrusion. I decided it was manageable for one trip anyway. I tried all of the ointments, but nothing worked.

I couldn't remember which shoulder it was that I had popped out of joint during a stupid fight, years back before the service. My parents had taken me to the hospital the following morning to get it checked out. I lied and told them it had happened while playing tackle football that morning. It was the second time I'd lied to them about an injury I received from acting stupid and horsing around.

From time to time for years afterward, the shoulder was very painful. In fact, I had gone to the doctors in the service, and more X-rays showed that a small bone chip from that fight was causing the shoulder to pop-out and cause severe pain. I sat before a group of military doctors who discussed the possible surgery needed. It would limit how far I could lift my arm by many degrees. Nah, that wasn't for me. Thank you, sirs, for checking it out. So sorry for wasting your time. I didn't want the limitation or the hassle of having the left or right shoulder cut into and repaired. I was still able to do the required eighteen pull-ups and climb the rope with my legs extended out in front of me, using only my arms. Those were my finest days of good health and vigor!

At the end of my time in the marines, I was a buff 148 pounds, with defined muscle tone on my arms and legs and a six-pack stomach. I ran like a deer, passing all of the physical fitness tests near the top.

Today, I can't even imagine doing *one* pull-up. It doesn't really matter, as both shoulders now have arthritis. However, I am doing a kind of push-up exercise by holding onto the kitchen or bathroom counter, extending my legs and arms out and then coming down on the counter and pushing back up—fifteen times, several times a day.

The end of summer had arrived and my fishing buddies came up to our little house for another three days of fishing. They were going to help me with power-washing and staining the large wood patio and stairs. It was just the three of us on that trip. Rick brought along his new, beautiful Triton bass boat. My bass boat, which I'd bought from him, was already there in the garage, ready to go. I had redesigned the original carport into a closed garage where we could safely park the two bass boats.

We went out on the boats, and the small of my back began to hurt. The other two guys were in Rick's boat, and I followed them in mine. It was fun on that early morning as we took off across the lake from our local ramp. The water was smooth as glass as we headed to a line of bass-filled tulles awaiting a short distance away. Rick had the hammer down and was moving along at more than sixty-five miles per hour. I was following and began falling behind his boat, hitting the waves and rolls as the wind picked up. The waves were not severe, but it became rough enough that with each up-and-down motion, the small of my back just ached more and more.

We had a wonderful day of fishing and laughing. I followed along behind them as the day passed on into the afternoon. It was now time to head back, take a break, and prepare the deck for staining. The run back to the ramp was a smooth drive, as Rick again had the hammer down and took the lead, while I tried to keep up with his perfect trim. Clearly his 175HP, 2004 Triton was faster than his former 175HP, 1987 Ranger, which had become my own muscle car on water. My Ranger is plenty fast, I assure you; I've lost many hats, sunglasses, gloves, and other objects from not paying attention. It's serious driving on water, and I am not one to mess around. No beer or anything else for me!

I was feeling more and more pain in my back as the guys began power-washing. I puttered around the house while they spent a couple of afternoons on the deck. They decided to selflessly forego their last full day of fishing so they could help me work on the deck. These are just great guys. Actually, one of them is my son's uncle. What a pleasure it is to have them as my special friends. When it came time to begin staining the wood, I hurt so bad that I had to sit in order to move the brush up and down. Later that night, I couldn't get comfortable sitting on the couch while we were watching TV. Between my shoulder and back pains, I had one miserable situation going on.

The last day of our fishing trip came to an end, and later that afternoon the guys drove off to their homes over in Stockton. These two special friends have been fishing pals for over forty years, growing up together in the delta country. After they left, I tried to finish the stairs and a small area on top that still needed a coat. As I was painfully trying to finish the last sixteen steps, I was sitting and groaning with each movement. The pain was getting to be so bad in both areas that I was only able to get four steps done. I took more over-the-counter pain medication and packed myself up so I could leave for home.

Oh, I didn't mention that I had quit smoking just before this last trip with Mark and Rick in late August of 2006. I did really well, considering what I had given up. I remember that I endured all of that pain and still kept off the cigarettes. I had very little physical stamina, and my lungs had not cleared the way they had when I'd quit previously. I just chewed and chewed that nicotine gum. Since I wasn't buying cigarettes, it was so cool to finally have some extra money in my pockets for fishing tackle or for this and that. However, I began to be a little concerned about what was going on in my body. Cindy already knew something was wrong, and she let me know about it whenever she had the chance to remind me—which was always!

Less than a month passed, and my brother went up with me to fish for the last time that year. This would be the last year I would be anything like my normal self. We spent three days in fishing bliss. My shoulder and back hurt like hell, but the fishing was great, and the company was even better! I was still off the smokes—except that I did sneak one out of my brother's pack while he took a shower, but that was the only time. He didn't know I took it, but considering that he was smoking around me all weekend, one last smoke was not so bad.

Smoking is such a social activity with other smokers. I look back and wonder how I had the will to not cave in and just say, "Oh, well, I'm going to let this be my last weekend smoking with my brother." I normally would've been looking for such an excuse, but I didn't. I was determined to make it that time, with the help of the gum and my strong will to finally give it up! That was the last fishing trip for the year, and everything after that time was going to drastically change in our lives. I hadn't personally met God yet, but that was coming.

By the way, I've been off cigarettes for well over five and a half years now. Going back to my previous figures, that's an additional savings of approximately $23,760.00. Where would I have come up with that money? Answer: an addict can and will find a way. That's too bad for the tobacco industry, for they lost a good customer. Those figures didn't include the thousands of dollars and cigarettes that Cindy has smoked or not smoked. She quit for good shortly after I did. So there you go, Big Tobacco. You're not getting any more of our money!

What Does God Have to Do with It? Everything!

You may have noticed that I haven't mentioned God much up until now. Well, I didn't need or appreciate Him for most of my life up until the really bad news came. Isn't that what most of us do? We wait until we really need Him—if we even believe that there is a God—and soon after He gives us a miracle or a blessing, we forget it and go on with our lives. I had continued to feed myself with whatever satisfied me—and maybe my wife, now and then. In other words, I got by with a minimal relationship with God, and I continually received a minimal return. As Dr. Charles Stanley said, "We reap what we sow, more than we sow, later than we sow." And I sowed many, many cigarettes.

It all started back in the fifties when I was a little guy being baptized a Catholic. Then I moved on to receive my first holy communion and confirmation, and I eventually married in the Catholic church for my first marriage. Every Sunday morning we heard our dad holler out those familiar words: "Get the door for your mother!" Then we drove in a smoke-filled car to and from church and wherever else we went that day, which was usually a ride to one of our grandparents' homes for a great Italian dinner!

My older brother and I would pass the hour or so in church looking at the backs of the heads of all the people sitting in front of us. Some of the head shapes and hair styles caught our attention. There was one man that we saw every Sunday for so long that I can still see him now. Every once in a while, we felt our dad's hand telling us to "knock it off!" for giggling or for a little horseplay. Church was so boring. I could never make out what the heck they were saying during the entire hour, and there was way too much echo. I'm sorry, but even today I can't hear a sermon because of the echo.

I knew who God and Jesus were, but I didn't really know much of anything, even after all those classes we were forced to take twice a week. It was enough to memorize the weekly stuff in order to get a star from our catechism teachers. My Mom was one of them, and I had no choice but to behave when our mom ran the class. What happened with most subjects was that we only memorized names, events, and stuff to keep it in our minds for a very short period of time. Then, after the many tests were over, the information was gone, evaporated, history. I remember that this happened in college when I took four art history courses over the years. We had to memorize hundreds of paintings, artists, styles, dates, and so on. Then, shortly after the exam, the information was forgotten, removed from memory. It was time to light up and move on.

In the sixties, my neighbor buddy and I were allowed to ride our bikes to church on Sundays. I think we may have gone there two times before we figured it out and turned our bikes in another direction. We headed around the block to our other friends' home. Their house was out of sight of our homes and our parents. They were brothers, and they had their own room in the back of the house. We had on our dress shoes and slacks, but under our jackets were nothing more than T-shirts.

Larry and I would park the bikes inside the gate in the back yard and go over to the brothers' window. Since it was early, we would grab a branch off the plum tree and stick it through a hole in their screen window. Hopefully, the glass window would be open, so we would only have to reach in there to awaken one of them and not the entire house. We were there to get our buddies going and to enjoy the breakfast that would surely follow. Their dear mom, not knowing of our shenanigans, would cook us up a great-tasting Sunday breakfast, well worth the diversion of going to church.

Until I met Cindy, I had no idea what kind of wreck I was spiritually. I knew a little of this and a little of that, but I was nowhere near where I am today in knowing God and following His Word. I have now committed my life to Him and Jesus Christ. To be with Cindy, I had to drop the *g-damn* word immediately. Coming from a punk hood with a know-it-all mentality, and being an ex-marine with a trashy mouth (not to blame the marines for any of this), I had to instantly change my terminology. I learned that by saying the *g-damn* word I was breaking the third commandment: "Thou shall not take the name of the Lord thy God in vain." This made perfect sense, and I dropped the saying I had used so frequently. When I hear profanity today, I am sickened by it—not to say that I don't slip from time to time. I especially can't stand hearing God's name used in vain.

Our marriage, her second and my third, combined her two older boys, which had fulltime, and my only son, of whom I shared joint custody. Cindy too came from a mainly Italian heritage; she was Catholic and taught catechism. We had both been born in San Francisco. Without her constant drive to keep God first and family second and to watch what we fed our minds, our lives together would not have worked. It's because of her initial love of Christ, yearning to keep Him first and have a closer relation with Him, that I am able to tell you my story today.

I fondly remember one time when both of my Italian grandmothers were at our house. It must have been in the mid-sixties. They were both in the kitchen, washing and drying the dishes from our Sunday dinner. Turning my back to them, I made my shoulder blades stick out. Oh, did I rattle the beehive! My dad's mom, my Noni (Italian for *grandmother*, as Cindy is called by our grandkids today), was so riled with my move that she started to go off into Italian, which caused me to laugh, which caused my other Grandma to say in English, "Stoppa doing that, Jimmy. God will keepa you like that." The commotion, started with my little prank, soon blew over, but that now-cherished memory of years past will remain with me forever.

No, I wasn't worried about God keeping me like that. However, many times when I got hurt or did something stupid, I would ask God for his help to heal or protect me. The prayers were sporadic, and the intensity of my asking the Lord for help was zip—nothing like it is today. There was a time in my young adult life when I didn't believe there was a God, and I felt that we had our own God inside us—which had nothing to do with the Holy Spirit. Stupid, ignorant crap came out of me, with virtually nothing going in that was worthy of a boy or man of God.

This gets back to what Cindy was always trying to teach us: that if we're not feeding ourselves with godly foods, we can't expect the treasures that God has in store for us. Without His Word, the Bible, we cannot expect, feel worthy of, or deserve His total goodness. It's taken many, many hours of pain, study, thought, reading, reflection, asking for forgiveness, talking to God, sharing gut feelings with my wife, and praying on our knees together in order to come through the many problems that have faced us yesterday, today, and tomorrow. I get it now, and now is never too late.

I have personally experienced God's miracles, even before my "big moment" of revelation. Most of my memories are from the time after I met Cindy. I can go back in my history and recall a variety of situations where God must have been there to get me through. However, I didn't remember them at the time, and I surely was never grateful for all of the things that He was involved with—which I now know was *everything*. And there we come, full circle.

Every marriage, every job, every opportunity, every friend and family member, every loss, every gain, every pain, every heartache, every love, everything has been a part of who I am now. God knew us before our birth and knows everything that is to come into our lives. Our journey is worth pursuing as long as we keep God first and trust Him with all of our heart. We can't go back and change a thing in our past, but we can see how every moment was put there by His divine design in order to prepare us for where we are in the present. The present is His gift to us now! Have we realized that God is the creator of the universe?

I now know that most everything that has happened and is happening to me was meant to be. I have free will and have been able to make my choices as I had wanted them to be. I've looked back at every opportunity that God has given me, from as far back as my early teens—and maybe an opportunity even before then. I can see back to when my neighborhood friend and I wanted to put on an act for the children at the Shriner's Hospital, when it was a short block away from my grandparents' house on 19th Avenue. If my grandmother had passed on the letter we wrote to their attention, would they have allowed us to perform? Would my acting and musical desires have been birthed that day? Why did I quit playing classical guitar after a year of lessons? Where would I be now? How come I didn't catch on to playing rock and roll? Why didn't I stay in the teaching profession or pass that police exam? After all, I was an MP, guarding Nixon's Marine One helicopter with a loaded gun.

Why did I sell my GTO and then pray for another one? Why did I hang around with the kids that experimented with alcohol and drugs? Why didn't I pursue my desires to be a zoologist, a scientist? If I had stayed in the Marines, would I have been promoted up the ranks to a Sergeant Major, E-9? I'd be retired now, but would I have been safe from harm's way? Would I still have gotten cancer?

Would I have a wife and family like I do today? Would I know God like I do at this moment? Would I be surrounded by miracles as I am today? When I got a job at a booming Silicon Valley telecommunications company before graduating from college, if I had stayed with it until this day, would I have been healthier or any better off, without worries of retirement or losing our home? If I had stayed married to my first wife, would we be happy today? Would I be better off? Would I be cancer-free? Would I know God? Would I have my name written in the Lamb's Book of Life?

If I had stayed with my picture framing store and kept building it for the last twenty-seven years, would I have been better off? Would my son's mom and I still have been married and our lives have been healthy and prosperous?

If I had not given up on a product, a concept, an idea that I had put my life into for well over twenty years, would I have finally made it? Would we be rich and all who believed in me have prospered as well? Would I have been hailed an overnight success? Did I stop three feet from the gold? When I first graduated from San Jose State, would I have gone on to earn a masters and then a PhD, as I desired?

The above were some of the many opportunities that God offered me along the way until now. I know why my choices, my decisions, my failures have brought me to where I am today. I had no God in my daily life. I flitted from one thing to another. Had I been a man of God, I would've had peace and a healthier life long ago. I was given many opportunities by my parents, but I chose to follow my friends—not that any of them were bad. I just didn't follow something that was in my heart. This long course of change, decisions, and selfish ways has finally brought me to this place where I am now. This is not my final destination but a point closer to where I know now that God originally knew I was going to be, which is where He wants me to be, with my beautiful wife whom I adore and cherish. As *The Whispers* sang, it "just gets better with time."

CHAPTER 2

Welcome to My Life of Cancer, Stage Four Lung

And All of the Strings Attached

After months of having no relief from the uncomfortable feeling in my left shoulder, my doctor finally sent me to an orthopedic specialist to have my shoulder further examined. He was an older doctor, more on the no-personality side, kind of stern looking. I needed some nice-guy stuff at this point: you know, upbeat, with a heart and some compassion. My regular doctor had a nice personality but missed some signs along the way regarding my care.

Anyway, the orthopedic doctor scheduled me for an MRI in late September of 2006, a week or so after meeting him. I think that was the first MRI I had ever taken, and I'd only heard the name once or twice before. After it was over, I never wanted to go inside one of those loud, claustrophobic, restrictive machines again. It was awful being stuck in that tube with the constant banging going on, and being so confined in something a mere inch or so above my face made the experience even more difficult. It took everything I had to get through that exam. If they could send a man to the moon, I thought, why couldn't they make a machine that was user-friendly and not so closed-in and terribly loud and constrictive? Why couldn't the machine play a selection of songs that the patient picked out? Some lullabies would be nice so that one could fall asleep.

A few days later, I went to the orthopedic specialist for a follow-up on the MRI. I arrived around four p.m. and was soon led into a darkened examination room. I sat there, kind of restless, waiting for

Dr. Personality to arrive. I had no idea that anything major would be wrong with my shoulder that some rest, a shot or two, or a painkiller couldn't take care of. I did think back to that fight years earlier, but it had been a long time ago, and I could now live without the pull-ups. I was completely in fantasy land.

What the doctor was about to tell me were the most shocking words I've ever heard. His nurse came in and stood in the background of the medium-sized examination room, and the doctor put the negatives on the light box mounted on the wall in front of me. I sat as the doctor started looking over the film. I watched him as he went from left to right and then stood back, saying aloud, "This is bad; this is real bad." Then he repeated those same words again, and his head shook from side to side: "This is bad; this is real bad." He definitely had my full attention. He went on to look at me and say, "You have cancer."

A cold, dark cloud came over me in that already darkened room. I immediately understood the word *cancer* and that he was talking about me. Then he starting pointing at my left shoulder and neck area and said that the cancer had metastasized and that it was all over. I didn't know what *metastasized* meant, other than that the cancer had spread. That was it; my cancer was spreading.

At that point, he finished shaking his head, turned on the overhead light, looked at me, and said that he was sorry. There was that compassion thing. Then he and his nurse guided me out into a full lobby where he said once again, "I'm sorry." I was oblivious to the other patients sitting and moving about.

My news wasn't good, but there was no consultation, no comfort to be found in that office. It was, as my grandfather used to say, "Putt-putt and good bye." I was now in the parking lot, walking to my truck, trying to grasp what I had just been told. I was still hearing him say, "This is bad; this is real bad." I thought, *What do I do now?* I immediately nicknamed him Doctor This-Is-Bad-Real-Bad.

It was a little before five p.m., and I thought about driving up the freeway to the next exit to go see my doctor, hoping that he was there for the open office hours that started at five. Sure enough, he was there, and one of his staff guided me to an empty little examination room and told me to wait, that the doctor would be right with me. I had been in these rooms over the years when another doctor had worked in this clinic. I really liked and missed that man. My wife and I had felt so comfortable with him. We are sure, to this day, that the other doctor would have caught my cancer and begun treatment much earlier. But then—and I just thought about it right this second—would I have met the same oncologist that we believed the Lord had anointed and guided to me? I'll explain shortly how we met.

I remembered the times I'd had diverticulitis and vertigo and high blood pressure skyrocketing into the 190s. And there was the time I'd had to take a shorter version of a colonoscopy in one of these examination rooms. I had acted so vain then—especially when two cute medical assistants moved in and out of the room, preparing things for the procedure. I had asked them, "You're not going to be in here when the doctor starts, are you?" They'd answered yes, and I went on to say, "Since the doctor is such a great Catholic man, can't he get an older nun who's a nurse to assist him?" I had been utterly embarrassed, wishing it was only a dream, as I was about to have them see my bare ass and partial plumbing.

As I sat there thinking about past medical procedures, my doctor came into the room, and we said hello to one another. I said that I had just come from the orthopedic specialist he'd sent me to. I went on to tell him what the specialist had said about my shoulder and all of the cancer. Then my doctor said, "I'm sorry, Jim. I've been away the last couple of weeks and was thinking of a way to tell you that you have lung cancer." I followed up with, "You just came out and said it. Wow!" After that, we really didn't discuss a plan, other than sending me on to a pulmonary doctor.

I called my high school buddy—or he called me—and I told him the news as I headed home to tell Cindy. It became a comforting conversation for both of us, as he told me of something serious that was going on with him too. After talking with him, I drove up our driveway, parked, and went inside. Cindy said, "I knew there was something seriously wrong with you months and months ago. I told you."

I just knew, and never thought for a second otherwise, that she would be with me through what was about to come. There is nobody more loving than this lady. If I were going to reincarnate into a pet, I'd want to come back as hers. I'm not saying that I didn't have the very best parents in the world; it's just that I've seen Cindy in action with someone in the hospital, doing anything she could to help or be of comfort. Cindy has a remarkable, loving heart, and I've been so blessed to have her as my wife and life partner.

I knew before my illness—and I've been reassured after it—that we will remain married till death do us part. With all of the baggage we both brought into this marriage, we've been tested many times, but we've always pulled through. Here was yet another test, one that was life threatening and would soon require a whole new spiritual outlook on my part. Cindy had the knowledge and total belief to help me know what I must do and exactly who I must go to for help, if I were to come out of this nightmare alive. This has become my new life—all day, every day, from here on after: I want to get to know God and Jesus and read and study the Bible and pray.

Meet Doctor Doom

It was the day of my appointment to meet with the pulmonary doctor. I drove over to his office before starting my new day on the road in sales. I remember him always smiling. That would usually be a good thing, but in this particular instance, it wasn't. We met, and I followed him into an examination room. He listened to my lungs, and I soon found out that there was only one lung working at that point. After he examined me, he went on to schedule me for a look inside and an examination at the hospital. This would require Cindy to take me in and bring me home. After setting the appointment, I went on with my work day, telling a few friends and customers what had recently been found.

I don't remember anything from the day that Dr. Doom probed around inside of my lungs. As I was coming out of the deep sleep, Cindy got the news of just how bad my condition was. After I came to, we left for home without Cindy reporting anything that she learned. Instead, she spoke with a positive attitude. That was just what I needed at that point—or at any point, right up until now. It's better for me. I don't want to know how long I have left, which is the standard question asked when a person finds out that they have cancer. There was just something inside of me that didn't want to know. That kind of news can start the tailspin down for many. In my case, I'm going to fight like hell to stay here.

We went back to see this doctor in a little room that reminded me of a salesman's office at a used car dealership. Cindy and I were sitting next to each other, looking out through the blinds at a highway that cut through town, and Doctor Doom sat across from us at a desk like one found in some cheap sales office. Cindy had taken time off from the café she had opened across the freeway from where we were. It was a booming business with a great staff that was able to cover her during her absence. I had just used a vacation day from my sales job for this appointment.

I thought to myself, *Boy, I didn't stop smoking soon enough. Now I'm sitting here, waiting to learn my fate.* Doctor Doom walked in with his usual smile and sat with his back to the window. He went right into the news, suggesting that we needed to get our stuff in order, that I had maybe six to nine months left. After his initial biopsy, he had told my wife that I had three to six months left. He said that we should travel, do things that I (we) had always wanted to do. "Get your stuff in order," he said. I guess that Doctors Doom and Gloom have to cover their asses.

There was nothing like, "I'd fight like hell. Are you a believer? Do you believe in God? Do you pray, and do you have family and friends who will pray with you or for you? And you should drink and eat thus-and-so." These kinds of responses would be excellent tools to fight this illness. I know, doctors can't get personal like that, mostly because of malpractice issues, or maybe they would feel that they're giving a patient false hope. But for God's sake, you'd think that after hearing that you have only a few months to live, such things would be the weaponry one needs to go up against a dreaded and deadly disease.

Doctor Doom wrapped it up by leading Cindy and me out into the lobby with the usual "sorry" and a big smile. He ordered me an array of oxygen tanks for all occasions—and I mean for *all* occasions. Having only one functional lung was not going to get me by. I still had no plan for treatment or an idea of where to go from there. This was back in the very beginning of October 2006.

The tanks arrived. I didn't like the looks of this. The hall closet was quickly filled with these creepy tanks, and the largest one had to stay out in the dining room. I was breathing just fine, but on their little meter, I was below what was good.

One tech in particular was simply pesty. He was friendly enough, but he'd show up at our door after six p.m., not calling ahead to ask if he could come over, which bugged us. He'd always come in and put the mask on me, no matter how good I was feeling. I was not going to carry around one of the many tanks that had been delivered for all occasions. It was a nice precaution, but in my battle plan, it wasn't going to happen.

I was determined to get all the tanks out of there. I asked the tech about it, and he said that I would have to be tested at night. Yeah, right. I called the doctor's office, and they said it was the doctor's orders. "He's not my doctor!" I replied. We had a co-pay for these tanks that was now over two hundred dollars. I made another call to the billing company and said that I didn't even use them and that I'd been overbilled. I went on to say that I wanted them out and that Dr. Doom was not my doctor.

I was fuming, especially after Cindy recalled the way that Dr. Doom had talked to her after the exploratory testing. He had come into the waiting room and asked for her and then said, "Everything went okay. Can we talk?" They walked out into the hallway, where he planted his foot up against the wall and confirmed the bad news to Cindy. She had immediately thought, *Look at this guy, standing there with that posture.* She had thought he was leading her into a private room for a conference. Instead, he just casually told her that her husband had three to six months at best. He went on to say, "I've seen this stuff before," casually standing there like they'd just run into each other in the hallway at the office. "Hey, wa's up? Oh, by the way, your husband has three to six months to live."

Pain was rising in my shoulder, and it began shooting down my leg into my thigh as well. It was excruciating and started to affect my ability to drive. By the end of that week, I had to call in to the office for a day or two off. It was Friday, and all I could do was try to find a comfortable position to sit or lie down on the family room carpet. A dear friend soon learned of my condition and the pain I was experiencing and came over with some fresh lemon-lime juice to drink.

On Sunday and I was again on the family room floor, trying desperately to find a position with the least pain. My primary "didn't-care" doctor hadn't bothered to follow up, and Cindy was upset with his lack of care. There was no excuse, even of having too many patients to give a darn. I do remember one time that I asked him to write a phony prescription to show my wife, telling her to have more sex with me for health reasons. It was funny, and at that time I was just in his office for something minor. I certainly thought that he was going to be my doctor for years to come.

Sunday evening led into Monday morning with the pain growing worse. Cindy had to leave for a short while that morning, so she had her sister come over to be with me. I had her sister massage my left thigh, which helped lower the pain level a bit. I hadn't slept the night before and was just exhausted. I laid out on the family room floor with an array of pillows around my body, as my sister-in-law continued massaging my leg. When Cindy got back home late that morning, she decided to bring me to the hospital for emergency help.

When Cindy, her sister, and I arrived, they had to get a wheelchair in order to get me inside. The pain persisted until I was registered and brought into a private room on the third floor. A variety of nurses and aides came in, and soon I was in a gown and hooked up to a bunch of tubes. One of those was the painkiller morphine. I had only heard of that drug in war movies where soldiers had to go on morphine when their limbs were blown off or they had been shot up. There were charts posted on the walls with a series of faces showing various pain levels numbered from one to ten. This became my friend, as I hate pain and could tell the nurse my exact level, so they knew what to do and how much to give me.

After a short time, my pain level went down to the third and second face, then back up not long afterward. It was time for dinner, and I was given my ration. I think Cindy, who hadn't left my side, went down to the cafeteria. I still had not seen any doctor, let alone my own. The food was . . . well, let's say: appreciated. There I was, unable to believe what had happened to my life.

Cindy had the duty of calling certain family members and friends. She would be off work for a while. Like I mentioned before, Cindy had a really good crew who could run the café in her absence. She kept busy, calling in for messages and updates throughout the day, and calling family and friends up into the night. She made a bed out of a reclining chair and was given an extra blanket and pillow, since she wasn't leaving my side.

My bed was alongside the windows and looked out across a neighborhood there in Vallejo. She closed the blinds, and we watched TV as we tried to sleep. Every ten to fifteen minutes, a nurse would come in and check me out. I had so many tubes coming out of my hands. I think I had oxygen as well. Thank God I didn't smoke at the time; I had quit months earlier. I was chewing the nicotine gum, which fortunately curbed my desire to smoke. I was so blessed that I didn't have to go cold turkey when I had to be admitted without any choice.

The following morning, my breakfast was delivered, and Cindy went downstairs to the cafeteria. In the meantime, I was given more morphine to kill the pain and whatever else was needed to keep my vitals where they should be. There had still been no contact with a doctor, to my knowledge. Cindy came back up to my room and sat with me as I lay there dozing off. Before I knew it, my lunch was served. I was now groggy, not really remembering being hungry or even eating for that matter—except that I had indigestion, so I must have eaten. I just wanted to go back to sleep.

Cindy said that she wanted to go home to take a shower and change, and then she'd come right back. We lived about eleven miles from the hospital. I barely heard her, but I knew she was leaving as I turned over and faced the window with the open curtains on that gray October morning.

Do you believe in miracles? Do you believe in guardian angels? God's grace? Do you believe in God and His Son, Jesus? Do you believe what I'm sharing with you? It is a true story. This story really happened, or I would not be here to tell it to you.

As Cindy started to drive out of the hospital parking lot, she heard a voice, saying, "Go back." She continued to drive on, heading out onto the main road, when she heard the voice again, telling her to "Go back." Cindy drove farther, heading toward the intersection where she would need to turn left toward the freeway, when she heard the voice again telling her, "Go back." She finally turned and headed back to the hospital, never making it home to take a shower and change her cloths.

(My wife always looks good to me. My comeback is always, "I'd take you to my reunion and show you off!" Her reply is always, "Nah, you're just saying that because you want something." However, this time I'd thought, *Not really, my dear. not in this condition.*)

She parked her car and headed back up to my room on the third floor. My door was closed as she walked in. Cindy immediately heard me gagging and rushed over to see me turning a purple color. She quickly ran back out into the hallway, calling out for help.

A "rapid response" call was soon heard over the intercom system, as every available nurse and doctor converged on my room. As I was being intended to, I could hear one voice in particular, calling out my name. I was down in a very deep, cold chamber, coming out slowly, awakening, trying to get a hold on where I was and what was going on. As I began to make out some of the many people around me, they were turning my bed around and heading me toward an elevator. From there I came to a room with an odd shape and things all about. It did not look like a regular room that I was accustomed to.

I was immediately hooked up to a bunch of machines, and I dozed off and on. I was down in ICU. Awhile later, I was reunited with Cindy, the lady who, with the guidance of our Lord, had just saved my life. She told me what had happened and then went on to tell her story of being told to "go back" to my room. Cindy had been told by the divine power of God to go back, and she had done so by God's grace. Do I have your attention now?

CHAPTER 3

Meet the Good Doctor, My Oncologist

They continued to check me out while I was in ICU. I was hooked up to oxygen and tubes that were giving me a little of this and a little of that. I was stuck with needles many times here and there. I hadn't had the port installed in my chest yet. I'd fall into a deep sleep, and then they'd wake me up for something else throughout the day and night. I was told that I not only had a collapsed lung but I now had pneumonia. From time to time a person would give me some kind of breathing test or something like steam or smoke coming out of a tube. I didn't have all my functions working normally yet.

I was in a weird area of the hospital, trying to figure everything out where I was and what they were doing to me. I remember seeing my daughter-in-law come into my room for a short hello. Some very special friends came immediately to the hospital to check up on me and to see Cindy. I greatly appreciated their concern, but I wasn't ready to visit with anyone else at that time.

I was in and out of sleep until the following morning when I saw these two men walk into my room, one of them holding a clipboard and both wearing the typical white coats with ties. One of them was an Asian man who seemed to be in charge. The other was a Caucasian fellow that kind of reminded me of a young Michael Douglas. Apparently, he was a student from the local medical college, Toro University, who was following the doctor around.

This particular doctor seemed to be very nice and seemed to have taken control of my situation immediately. To my knowledge, I still had not had a doctor check me out or assume control over my situation. Up until this time, it seemed that I only had the one "primary didn't-care" doctor. This new doctor seemed to be very concerned, aggressive, and ready to begin treating me with chemotherapy the very next day. I liked this doctor immediately and felt his confidence and caring nature. It seemed that we finally had a plan to get going on this cancer thing. Do you think this might have been that "divine design" stuff again? I believe now that this doctor was anointed, chosen by God to heal me. I tear up about it even now as I write. I am so blessed to this day, and less than twenty-four hours ago I had the privilege of hugging him after my recent check-up.

I soon compared my oncologist to an art history teacher I'd had in junior college because of the kindness he showed to me. My art history teacher would say, "Good Morning, Jim," as he entered the large-forum classroom. I was waiting outside—you guessed it—smoking. I sat in the forum as he showed slides, and if I ever raised my hand, he called on me by name, saying, "Yes, Jim." It made me feel so special that I said to myself, *I am going to give this teacher an A*. I would study extra hard for his kindness shown to me.

I have told my oncologist this story, comparing that teacher to him. My oncologist made me feel special; therefore I was going to be one of his especially good patients and win my battle with cancer. It's been over five years now since we met down in ICU and he took me on as his patient. Do you see what power an act of kindness can have? Listen up, negative doctors and patients, family members and friends.

Look for the special people that God will bring into your life if you have Him in yours. At a minimum, know who God is and how great He is and have absolute respect for Him; for He knows where you're going, and He's known since before you were even born. It's this full-circle thing that I have talked about.

I was brought back to my original room the next day, but before that, they had me wait temporarily in another room with another patient. Cindy was with me when a well-dressed lady walked in and introduced herself as the CEO of the hospital. My good friend and mentor was on the board of directors, and I think he had mentioned that I was a patient there. Boy, things were looking up. It was such a great pleasure to meet her, and I was truly honored that she had taken a moment of her time to come and see me. I believe I heard that she is proactive and gets around to meet patients, just as Cindy goes around to the tables in her café to say hi and to thank the customers for coming in to eat. There's such power in treating customers or patients as if they matter, because they do!

It was Wednesday, and I was to begin that mysterious process called *chemo*. All I knew was that you lost your hair and got really sick. Again, let me tell you how glad I was that I had quit smoking. I only had a few urges for a piece of nicotine gum once in a while. I was losing my desire and taste for tobacco with every day that passed.

The only other time I had stayed in a hospital was way back when I was a junior in high school and tried to pull off some shenanigan while horsing around one night. Back in those days you could smoke, at least in particular areas in the hospital. There were actually a couple of other times when I had stayed overnight in a hospital for my tonsils and for minor surgery on the inside of my lip.

A really nice nurse came in to set me up with my first chemo drip. The fact that the nurse was so sweet took much of my fear away. It lasted three to four hours and it was no big deal—yet. This was just the beginning.

A couple of waitresses stopped by to visit with Cindy and to see how I was doing. That was a nice afternoon. I was still receiving morphine for the pain in my leg. It wasn't as bad, but it was still there. The nurses were extra careful, now, giving me that particular painkiller. Everything was okay, and I had no hard feelings about the accidental overdose and who may have authorized the amount that almost gave me an earlier "check-out time."

On Thursday, it was the same routine with the chemo, and the same sweet nurse came in and gave me the drip. The tops of my hands were looking pretty punctured from the different procedures that I was receiving thus far. They had plans to take care of that in the upcoming days. The oncologist would have a "drip port" installed in the upper right portion of my chest. That way it would be much easier for them to rig me up for the chemo drip instead of continually punching into my veins. They still use that same old port today.

Nothing happened, so far as any hair falling out. I could still eat, and I had an appetite. Then Friday came, and that was the day I was to be discharged later in the morning, after my third chemo of the first session. One of the nurses scheduled me for a PET scan over in Walnut Creek and then worked very hard with Cindy on my discharge plans so that she could get me over there on time for the test. This happened to be the other sweet nurse, the one I'd first heard and then seen as I was coming out of that deep, cold place during the overdose.

The third chemo of the first session was now over, and Cindy helped me get cleaned up and dressed. I felt pretty good at that point and very optimistic. I don't remember seeing my oncologist that morning, and I hadn't seen my regular "didn't care" doctor since he'd given me the news about my lungs having cancer—after all that time treating it as an allergy. The discharge papers and prescriptions were ready. The nurse who did the scheduling emphasized the importance of washing our hands often, because I was now susceptible to the rotten stuff that comes from bacteria, people, and life in general. We were told again to wash our hands all of the time.

My chariot arrived on time, and we were quickly brought down the elevator and out to the pickup/drop-off area in front of the hospital. Cindy left me in the chair as she went to get her car. I just sat there and, if anything, took a large breath in and blew out a sigh of relief. I was going home, sweet home.

It was late morning when Cindy drove us over the bridge and down into Walnut Creek. The entire plan, from my standpoint, was to get this test over with before the weekend-getaway traffic began to jam the toll bridge, getting us stuck in traffic. At that point, I just wanted to go home. I was feeling pretty good, compared to where I had been only a few days ago.

We spotted the building, found a place to park, and headed to the elevator and up to the floor for the exam. Cindy sat outside in the lobby, probably making calls and reflecting on all of the stuff that she had just gone through. She was fielding calls from many friends and family who had begun to hear about our situation.

I was now in a room where I was to rest, while the stuff they had me drink worked its way throughout my body. That lasted for about an hour, while my mind was busy thinking about where I was. After the wait, I was led into the room with the PET scan machine. This is the machine where a number of little pets are spun around in a chamber or cage to look for hot spots where cancer could still be in the body. I am just kidding. I thought the name of this machine—along with the (kitty) CAT scan—were kind of nutty, and I always tried to keep a good sense of humor going.

I have a thing about names like *artichoke* and *Petaluma*. I have driven my wife and family crazy—and I mean crazy—over the years with these stupid stories that I've come up with. I had better warn Cindy about this section of the book so she doesn't tear the pages out as she proofreads them. Or maybe I'll just hide these few lines, since I know they will get her going. Anyway, for example, *Petaluma*, California, got its name because, in the old days, people in San Francisco would take the ferry and coach out to the country to see and pet the now-extinct *lumas*. These were large and very gentle animals that originated off the coast of Sonoma County. They were much like the gentle llamas of South America. When asked where they were headed or coming back from, they would often reply, "We're going (or we went) to pet the lumas."

I also told the story of how artichokes got their name. You have probably already figured that one out. "Poor Old Arty . . ."

Then there was *Antioch*, named after Och, a lady that came from the Netherlands and settled along the Sacramento and San Joaquin Rivers in Contra Costa County. She and her large family immigrated to the West Coast, where she got into the local politics and the fishing industry. She was beloved by all and was fondly referred to as "Auntie Och" by the children and elders in their community. Now you can put "the rest of the story" together.

It's silly stuff like this that can hold my sanity together while all the bad stuff goes on around and through me. I may draw out a chuckle or "We've heard that story before, and it's dumb!" from others—including the occasional believer who says, "Really?" My mind doesn't want to think about or remember the names of cancer-killing chemo drugs or this or that med. Just try to KISS life with what works for you.

The PET scan (don't get me going on the word *pet* again) was completed on time so we could reach home on the other side of the bridge before the rush of people getting away for the weekend. It was amazing how well we were moving along.

I knew the roads all around us very well, since I traveled on them every day up to 3,500 miles a month. I'd drive an average of 140 to 300 miles in a day. I just loved being out there, especially when I could smoke. I hadn't been off cigarettes long enough to avoid thinking about them often.

All I had then was the nicotine-laced gum. Actually, I was down to the two-milligram level, coming down from the maximum of four milligrams. I'd chew around twelve pieces a day. The flavor gave me the good breath that I always wanted to have when meeting with our customers—or any time. Now people couldn't smell me from out in the parking lot. One set of customers used to tell me that they could smell me out in the parking lot before they ever saw me come into their store. I'd had no idea that the smell was that offensive. Fortunately, they liked me, or I would never have been allowed to call on them.

After I finally quit, I was no longer the rep who smelled like smoke. I did take an extra precaution and always sprayed myself with a little cologne before going in any store as well. Why didn't I just listen to my dear mom many years ago? She'd say, "You reek of smoke!" Now I knew what she meant, except now it was too late, as I had lung cancer—stage four to boot—just like my dear ol' dad.

Cindy drove us across the bridge and through the main junction where two major freeways merged. I could see our housing development off in the distance and knew that we'd be home soon. We pulled into the driveway, and I got out of the car with Cindy's help. I was now pretty weak, but I surely felt much better than I had just a week earlier.

We got inside, and I knew that we both felt relieved. She immediately went over to the kitchen sink to wash her hands, and I headed toward the stairs with my bag. Cindy looked over and asked where I was going. I told her that I was heading upstairs to get my sweats on and was then coming back down to sit in the recliner. Cindy said that she was going to pick up my medication.

I looked over at the recliner that I was looking forward to relaxing in. I put my left hand on the oak banister and my right foot on the first step and held my bag in my right hand. I looked over at Cindy, heard the water running in the sink, and started to go upstairs—when I immediately lost my balance and heard a cracking sound.

I began to swing around to my left, while still holding on to the banister. I thought that I was literally breaking the oak banister off the wall. I swung around to the left and then stopped and got my balance. When I got my thoughts and bearings back, I looked at the banister. It was still perfectly intact. I did feel something strange about my shoulder, though, and it began to hurt. I sat back down on the first step.

Cindy was drying her hands as I called over to her at the sink. "Call 9-1-1. I just broke my shoulder."

She looked over at me and asked, "What?"

I said, "It's all going to work out for the best. Everything's going to be okay."

"What's going to work out for the best?" she asked.

I answered, "I think I just broke my shoulder. Call 9-1-1." I stayed calm, not really believing what had just happened.

Cindy made the call, and medics and firemen showed up in force at the house. I had seen some of these guys around Safeway as they shopped for the meals they ate at the fire station. There I was, heading right back to the place we had just left earlier that day.

I could see Cindy driving her car right behind us, as I was laid out in the ambulance looking out toward her. I couldn't believe it. I had been so close to lying in the recliner, watching TV in our own home. I don't remember if the siren was sounding, but we were heading right back to the hospital. The traffic going the opposite direction, which we had avoided, was the typical bumper-to-bumper traffic going toward Sacramento, Reno, and Lake Tahoe every Friday afternoon.

I thought about what had just happened and how fortunate I was that it hadn't happened several weeks earlier when my brother and I were out on the boat for the last time of the season. He had come up to our little house, known as "the lodge," for three days of fishing and to help me with some other projects that I needed to do. I could see myself, bending over the haul in order to hook up the chain to the pulley on the trailer, while my brother had us backed into the water so we could trailer up. Thank God that there had been no crack *then*—like the one I tried to explain earlier—from the pressure I had put on my shoulder to crank the boat up. Wow. I thank God. What a mess that would've been! See? It could've been so much worse!

Instead, we had gone out and caught many bass and released them all. After fishing, he helped me finish staining the deck. There had been a little unfinished patch remaining on the top section, and I still had some steps to do on the stairs. I don't remember having a bunch of pain that particular weekend, but of course I still had that mysterious, painful bump on top of my shoulder. And I had pain in the small of my back. At that point, 800 milligrams of Motrin had seemed to calm down the pain, especially while I fished. We got the painting done and had a wonderful time out on the lake. That would be the last trip to the lodge for a good while. My brother smoked the entire time, except inside my truck and inside the lodge. I did ask myself why I had quit before our last time out on the boat fishing, as it was such a relaxing thing to do, but I am glad that I had quit.

The reason I brought up this particular trip is that it was the last time I would trailer up the boat prior to shattering my shoulder. I want to emphasize this situation again. My brother always sat in my truck and positioned the trailer down the ramp so I could drive the boat up onto it. I'd drive the boat up onto the rubber rollers and, with the engine still running, I'd go up to the bow, get down on my knees, and bend and reach over the short railing in order to clip the hook from the trailer onto the boat. Then, with the left hand and arm, I'd grab the handle, apply pressure as I cranked down on it to take up the slack, and secure the boat on the trailer.

What if my shoulder had busted up then from the strain and pressure of winding? It was the perfect time for the shoulder to crack, just as it had when I grabbed on to the banister to go upstairs. What a mess that would've been! Thank you, God, for getting me home safely from that fishing trip with my brother. That trip had been just a few weeks earlier than now—when I was lying in an ambulance with a cancer-loaded, busted-up left arm. See? It somehow did work out for the best. I hadn't known at the time that I was full of cancer!

We arrived in the emergency department, and I was brought into a small room for an examination—and then off to take an excruciating X-ray or two. It was so painful getting the X-rays and being manipulated around so they could get the best pictures. I don't remember being offered any pain medication.

It was now evening, and my fishing brother and his wife came up to see us. It was an effort for them to drive all the way up from Gilroy that early on a get-away-weekend evening. While my dear wife had followed the ambulance, she had been notifying family and friends what had just happened. I can't imagine what was going on in her mind at that point, watching me go through all of this as I came apart piece by piece. All I know is just how blessed I am to have her as my wife and to have her here with me. This makes me stop and reflect on the marital saying "for better or for worse." She adds, "But I'm your wife, honey." Now there's another welling in my eyes.

Stop and think, though, just how much worse things could have been. This, in the grand scheme of things, was nothing. I guess I always look at what happened to me as nothing, compared to how awful it could have been. I am being protected. I still had all of my body parts, and everything seemed to be working well—except my shoulder . . . and my lungs . . . and then there's my back. Okay, but still, things could be so much worse. It is so important to never, ever forget this!

Let me mention here about my back. The CAT scans, MRIs, and PET scans to come would determine that both my third and fourth vertebrae were loaded with cancer—hence the severe pain that ran down my left leg. The doctor who put my left shoulder back together insisted to my oncologist that I should have my back repaired at another hospital. My oncologist, who was the commanding general in my battle, did not see that as something I needed. He said no to the idea, and thank God for that. I couldn't imagine going through major back surgery at the same time all of this was happening—or *ever*, for that matter. My oncologist planned to treat that area with the chemo and radiation that was forthcoming.

There was nothing further for them to do in emergency, so I was taken to another private room upstairs. They had scheduled surgery for the following morning. I could barely move without extreme pain. Later on that evening, Cindy left with our sister-in-law to go home, freshen up, and try to get some rest. They would return in the morning.

Meanwhile, my brother stayed with me for the night. He had to make do, sleeping in a padded chair, and he had to wear latex gloves and hold a urinal up to my little guy while I peed. I was so glad that he was up to the job. Cindy would be my first and only choice, but under these circumstances, my brother would have to do. I couldn't imagine a nurse for this procedure, man or woman.

See what a jerk I am? Give me an older Catholic nun anytime, and then I'd maybe feel comfortable. That's what I've always told Cindy about who I'd accept to give me a massage. No men or women, thank you very much. Later, Cindy would be put to the test of just what she would do for her husband. Thank you, honey!

Having my brother there or anywhere was always fun. We have this thing about us, where we can just talk to talk. I have another pal like that. My brother will usually drive me nuts first, but it's all in fun, and it's who we are. We've had some laughing sessions where we would just laugh uncontrollably.

I think during that time in the hospital my primary "didn't-care" doctor finally made his appearance. He came into my room that evening, made some joking comment about me returning so soon, and then left. I don't believe that I have heard of or seen him again to this day.

My oncologist did come by, and I saw him more during those painful days than my primary care physician. Maybe my primary care doctor just gave up on me when he predicted that I wouldn't make it through all of this. I didn't mean much to him, and to this day he has never made contact with me. Nor have the other naysayers. It's just as well, since I don't want to be around those negative guys. In my earlier life, I naively thought that all doctors were good, like any other highly regarded professionals—lawyers, dentists, or even politicians! I'll change my feelings someday and go by their offices to show them what God and His Son, Jesus, will do when you have faith in them and their supernatural powers. For I have learned and now believe that "nothing is impossible with God." I know that Doctors Doom and Gloom understand truism, but they can't say so, or they might be liable for being positive during these negative times.

The morning came, and I was soon being prepared for surgery. I was painfully transferred onto the gurney and wheeled on down to where they'd put my shoulder back together. See, this is a good part again: I had a shoulder that they could put back together. Something worse can always happen, and we can come up with a short list that can make you say to yourself, "Thank you, God, for giving me an arm that will still function, with a hand and five fingers too!"

To this day, as I type, my shoulder feels so good and normal. However, I won't even try a push-up or any other activity that could in any way jeopardize just how good it feels. I can raise it, fish with it, sleep, steer the wheel, and lift. How blessed I am!

I have my shoulder—the same one that Doctor Oh-This-Is-Bad-This-Is-Real-Bad saw as he looked over my MRI. Back then, he escorted me out into the lobby, and I left his office, never to see him again. That kind of repeated negativity can become fuel for the spirit to fight back, as you will see.

I was anesthetized, and shortly afterward they cleaned out my shoulder full of cancer and reconstructed it. After the surgery, as I was being wheeled into ICU, I had a kind of mystery movie going on in my head from being under, and I was the main character in this particular movie. It was so real to me. It took me a good while to shake the whole event from my mind. I started asking weird questions of the guy who was wheeling me to the area where I'd be staying while in ICU.

After that buzz was over, I saw Cindy and her sister, and then my youngest son came with his mother. It was a dismal Sunday in October. Between visits, I had an array of nurses and assistants checking me and tubes coming out of my arms. My pain level was finally under control, but I kept slipping back into that mystery scene I had been in.

Meanwhile, my wife got the unpleasant pleasure of meeting the surgeon and got a dose of his bad "bedside" manners. He got short with her as she asked him typical questions anyone would ask the doctor who had just put her husband's cancer-ridden shoulder back together. I wouldn't want to tangle with that old Irish tough guy, but he certainly was out of line, getting short with my wife. He later went on to apologize for his manners, but it really didn't matter; the damage had been done.

After a day or so in ICU, I was brought up into another single-patient room to recuperate. Cindy was by my side the entire time. My oncologist had discussed my condition with the surgeon. The surgeon went on to insist that I have my back taken care of too. The cancer was in my third and fourth vertebrae.

My oncologist didn't agree with major back surgery, as he thought there was a less drastic means of healing my back. Thank you, God, for your anointing of this oncologist!

The surgeon did do a wonderful job on my shoulder. He used some new hardware, I think he told me, from the Netherlands or somewhere over there. Thank you, God, for making a great orthopedic tool. It has never even set off an alarm at the airport. To this day it works, and I am able to do virtually anything I need or desire to do—and that includes fishing. As far as exercise goes, I can do push-ups off the counter but not off the ground, marine style. I am concerned about putting that amount of pressure on it. I never really lost weight throughout this entire cancer ordeal. I've been fortunate and gained and maintained a heavier weight. But now it's time to lose some weight and never find it again.

A physical therapist came in before I was to be discharged and gave me instructions on how to get my arm moving with some elementary movements. I was also very constipated and uncomfortable, which he helped me to resolve. Thank God that he helped me, because it was becoming way too painful. I won't go into details, but I owe him and Cindy for their help.

I am so grateful for his profession and for all the others that are there helping us through our time of need and not being concerned about all of the details that would creep me out. For that matter, I have tons of respect for just about all jobs, especially those that always seem to get downgraded—like flipping burgers, washing dishes, helping and cleaning up after people, picking our fruits and vegetables (as long as it's legal employment), and so on. All my life, I've lived with that respect. Do you really think it would be easy to stand behind the counter at a super-busy fast-food chain during lunch hour? That would be one of the last pressure cookers I'd ever want to be in. God, please bless them all.

Speaking of thanking God, I'm going to thank Him and my great oncologist again for not letting the other doctor go forward with back surgery. I've heard that back surgery is brutal and takes a long time to heal. Today, I am still limited in what I can lift; my limit is twenty to twenty-five pounds. This keeps me from doing many unpleasant jobs! To this day, I'll have a little lower backache after standing for long periods or bending over while weeding the yard. But 99 percent of the time, my back and shoulder feel good. My oncologist did order the radiation procedure, and he gives me a drip every other month to help strengthen my bones. The radiation that was provided by Dr. Gloom and his staff seemed to do the job that my oncologist was looking for. I am so grateful for that!

Hi, God. I'm Back, as You Knew I Would Be

We were finally home after an event that I never would have imagined. However, remembering that everything can always be much worse than it is, it didn't seem so bad after all. This would be my first time home in well over a week. It would be the first time I could relax, have some quiet time, and actually reflect on what we had been through and what we'd be facing. I didn't have the excruciating pain or the constant urges for more of the nicotine gum. I wouldn't be interrupted every ten minutes by someone just trying to do their job—which annoyed the heck out of me, especially when I'd finally fallen asleep.

Cindy was already out getting my meds and groceries shortly after we got home. I was now alone in my chair. It was pretty easy to get comfortable with only a sling on my left arm to hold my shoulder steady. I was able to put a little pillow where it would add comfort. I had the remotes and a small fishing-themed blanket for additional comfort. I was set, ready to relax. A small playpen was in front of me along one wall in our family room for our grandson. The TV was sitting directly above and in front of me on top of the fireplace mantel. Since it was chilly and we were in the midst of fall, it was sure nice to have that small gas fire burning.

I don't remember having the TV on as I began to think about all that had just happened over such a short period of time. My thoughts touched on where I might be headed. Some of the negative remarks filled my mind. Thanks, Dr. Doom. I hadn't met Dr. Gloom yet, the cake-topper! Anyway, I sat there in the recliner, alone in the house, and began to tear up and then to cry. I was afraid, very afraid, and I asked God to please forgive me for smoking and ruining the body that He gave me. "Please, God," I prayed. "Please, Jesus, forgive me. I want to stay here and not die. Please help me."

I felt a calmness come over me. Something was telling me—or I was telling myself—that I'd be here another thirty years. (Thirty was always a special number for me.)

But there I was again, asking God for help after not talking to Him, praying to Him, reading His Word, or appreciating all of my God-given blessings. I had done nothing since the last time I'd called for His help, yet he had answered me every time. I had forgotten Him afterward, as most of us do, and had gone on to the next time I needed Him, expecting Him to be there. I had more or less abandoned Him and His Son, Jesus, for most of my life, especially in the better times when my own free will ruled my life.

Reading the Bible was not in my cards. It was boring. Going to church was boring. Meanwhile, Cindy prayed all of the time and read her Bible. She would go to church and go on retreats to refresh her spirit. I had prayed from time to time, but only when I really needed help or wanted to please Cindy. God and His Son would answer some of the more common requests—or maybe it was just my imagination, as strange as that may sound. But He didn't answer my prayers and dreams as I asked, because I wasn't going about it the way that I now know. It took something as devastating as cancer for me to finally get to know God and His Son, Jesus. Again, all of it could've been worse—much, much worse—and you and I could come up with a long, painful list of what-ifs.

I began receiving many wonderful "get well" cards from customers, family, and friends. There were so many prayers being said on my behalf. I was facing a long battle with my cancer situation, and I took it day by day with a positive mental attitude.

My oncologist and his head nurse had it all scheduled out for the next five chemo sessions, which entailed three days in the chair with the drip. So I had fifteen more actual days, stretched out over the next three months. Mixed in with all of that were blood tests at an independent clinic and a long schedule of visits to the orthopedic surgeon—which always included an X-ray for the shoulder. At the end of the chemo would be the beginning of radiation, a follow-up for the cancer that was in my shoulder and vertebrae.

Do you know how blessed and grateful I was to have all of this treatment available for me, especially after I'd gotten myself hooked on cigarettes? I didn't take any of this for granted. I had been blessed by our Lord.

Now I must pay back for all of this. Hence, I hope that I am able to give you, the reader, something useful out of this book, something that will be of help to you, your family member, or a friend. I want to live and be here in order to give back. The prayers from others and from me are being answered as I go on believing in our Lord and having constant faith in His supernatural powers. Now that I'm looking back, I see that there were so many people involved in my healing, all provided by God and Jesus.

Shortly after I returned home from my first chemo session at the hospital, my long, brown, Italian, curly hair fell out. I loved that hair, full of mousse and hairspray that would withstand gale-force winds.

I went to our original café one particular morning, wearing my daily dress slacks, shirt, and tie. I was feeling and looking so good that I took a napkin and tore it into two pieces. Before turning around and looking at the large mirror behind me, I shoved the napkin pieces into my cheeks. I then turned around and looked at myself, holding my right hand and fingers together, Italian style. I gave myself a jeering look and said, "What are ya looking at, huh?" adding an Italian accent to it. I instantly scared myself!

My oldest stepson was visiting with me while Cindy was working at the café. That afternoon, I kind of pulled on my hair and out came a clump. This is a weird sensation to have happen, and many, many people have had this happen from a variety of illnesses. Ben kindly and generously went over to our neighborhood Walmart and bought a barber kit so he could shave my head. While he was away at the store, I went out into the yard and just began pulling it out and putting the hair into a plastic bag.

When Ben arrived back home, he put the cutter together and gave me a buzz cut like he and his brother wore. It came out good. There was some trimming here and there to do later to complete the "chemo" look. My brother ultimately came up and taught me how to shave my head for that "Kojack" look, which is very popular today.

I hadn't had my hair cut that short since my early days in the marines. At that point, I began wearing a Marine Corps ball cap. I figured, *What the that heck. Once a marine, always a marine.* This was my battle garb, and I later referred to God as my Commander in Chief and my oncologist as the Commanding General. I have this small tattoo on my right forearm that now faintly reads: USMC. Prior to being reborn a Christian, I always referred to it as my birthmark.

Unfortunately for me, I didn't lose much weight. It could always be found nearby. Now I wish that I could lose it, but back then weight loss was not a good sign. My sense of smell was on super-high alert, so many foods were not appealing. Thanks to my wonderful and patient wife, who kept me nourished with what would taste okay and stay down. There was only one time that I couldn't keep something down. Cindy had kept after me to try a particular food. I forget what it was, but I said no thanks, and she kept telling me to try it. I finally did, and that was it. She no longer gave me anything I didn't want to eat.

I had to face a crappy, lousy situation with the company I had loved working for since 1993, except for a couple of side tracks. I had been in the picture framing business for most of my adult life at various levels. I had worked at a frame store while working my way through my junior and senior years in college with the GI bill, where I found myself in art education.

Shortly after graduating, I found a teaching job. Then I received another job offer, but I had started my own framing business out of my home, which led to a venture with my older brother a year or so later, which then led to a full-time retail store. I managed it with several employees and was part owner; my brother did the books and kept me in business and out of trouble.

After a physical move six years later, I went back to being an employee because of an idea, an invention that I really let consume me—without God and depending on self-help business books and other related material. The hours upon hours that I spent on reading and research, without God, were taking me nowhere. I would have been so much further ahead and better off by reading and studying the Bible, listening, and praying to God and Jesus. Maybe, just maybe, I would have made it—or at least have achieved something sooner—if I hadn't stumbled around as the Israelites did during their forty-year journey that should have taken only eleven days.

My venture went on for twenty-plus years. Thinking back, I can see that I wasn't going to succeed without God's help, and I didn't. I went on to be a part-time framer in a mall and then started again on my own part-time business.

Later on, I was blessed with an opportunity to be employed as a sales rep for a major picture frame molding company from down in Carson, California. I mentioned earlier about driving many miles on my daily sales route over the years I was employed. I had the beautiful northern California territories from Carmel and Monterey up through the Bay Area, San Francisco, through the wine country, and at one time, on to Lake Tahoe, Truckee, Reno, and thereabouts.

I loved my job representing the company that employed me. I loved my coworkers, the owners, and the customers. This job gave me the most perfect opportunity to have my son at least half-time. My schedule was flexible enough to allow me to serve our customers within the same area where my son went to preschool and up. I would be able to pick him up and drop him off as needed throughout his school years, without interrupting my work responsibilities.

Now it had to come to an end. I had to resign as of October 31, 2006. I could no longer drive on a daily basis or do any of the physical activities required in that day-to-day employment. I didn't even smoke at that point. This was sad. The company had been so good to me over many years that I was finally content with who I was and what I did and would probably do for the rest of my working life. I was proud of everything I'd done as a sales rep. The job had made me do my very best, and I could've done even better.

I would've stayed with this company many more years had I not gotten sick. I guess I reaped what I sowed . . . more than I sowed . . . later than I sowed . . . don't you think?

CHAPTER 4

A Memory Just Arrived, and It's Here to Celebrate

Here it is in the middle of February 2011. A few years have passed since I sat in my reclining chair with that chemo feeling going through my body—as it does now once again. The cancer is back but not nearly as bad. There's a combination of feelings, smells, and taste. The great part of being able to sit here is that Cindy is sitting right alongside me in her own reclining chair, covered with a soft and cozy blanket, sipping her coffee, enjoying the heat from the gas fireplace.

What makes this setting extra special and extremely meaningful is that only a little over five years ago, Cindy and I would have been sitting outside the doorway in the garage. I would have had my big ass on a pickle bucket, and her much smaller rear would be on the carpet inside the door. It would be around 5:30 a.m., and both of our coffee cups would be brimming full of that hot, delicious drug, coffee. We'd both have freshly lit cigarettes in our mouths, breathing out smoke.

So what's the big deal about all of this? Well, today we are sitting close together *inside* the house, just as we did *outside* for many years, talking about the new day, yesterday, and what would be up for tonight. However, we are not smoking to our hearts' content.

Early morning often gave me a chance to think of where I was going and whom I'd be seeing for that day, as I'd be out on the road on my sales route in another hour or so. It was our special time for being together.

Well, that all came to an end—*thank you, God*—when I quit smoking only a month or so before the Big News that I'd been diagnosed with the lung cancer. Do you see just how addictive and wrong it was?

We were enjoying coffee, as we still do, and cigarettes as our special morning ritual. It was our breakfast, our power meal before starting the day. We wouldn't think of smoking in the house because of our sons and the odor that lingers. We just braved the cool weather in a place where we could smoke and drink coffee before it was time to get ready. I could not have imagined a better way to begin the day.

I smoked ten or eleven cigarettes, a mass of tobacco, before I even started on the road. I carefully counted them before going home at night to figure out if there would be enough for us to share the next morning. I never knew how many she had in her purse. All of this madness went on every single day. After leaving in the morning, I'd go get gas and more cigarettes for that day, which would lead into wondering if I had enough for the next morning—and so it went, each and every day. I am already dizzy just reading this!

Of course, this was dumb, and we were guilty of such disregard for our bodies and our Father who gave us these bodies. By having God in our lives and committing our lives to Him and Jesus, we are living differently now.

When Cindy comes down from her prayer room, and I come inside from my office in the garage, we sit in our respective recliners for our new morning ritual. Instead of going down into the garage to have our smoke and coffee, we now meet inside for our morning conversation—but with a twist. I read a daily devotional that I receive from Joel Osteen every weekday, and she shares what she has read earlier in her prayer room from Dr. Charles Stanley's Bible study or Joyce Meyer's daily devotional.

I hope that by now I have given you some kind of look inside my life, and you can see just how ignorant I was to have lived my life for so long without having God play the major role in my life.

This didn't change until my primary "didn't care" physician said those chilling words on that late afternoon in the beginning of October 2006: *lung cancer.* That happened just before I decided that I really wanted God and Jesus to become the major focus of my life. Now I need them. Please don't wait like I did.

CHAPTER 5

Now Meet Doctor Gloom

It was now March of 2007. After completing months of chemo, it was time to start the radiation for my shoulder and vertebrae. My oncologist referred me to a radiologist two cites up from his clinic, one that would accept my health insurance.

Cindy and I went to an appointment for a consultation of what the radiation was going to entail. We were both in good moods and great spirits. We entered the lobby and checked in. It was a nice, large office just off the freeway, so it would be easy for me to get there on my own. If I could scrounge up some extra spending money, this would be an ideal location, because at the exit prior to this one, there was a cool, new tackle store.

We were called into another small examination room and were told that the doctor would be right in. Cindy and I sat down, feeling so good. My spirits were high. This was a good sign, as I had come through my chemo battle against a collapsed lung and stage-four cancer with all that pain and all those side effects—not to mention a serious case of pneumonia.

Just then, Dr. Gloom knocked and walked in. He was a handsome, younger man with *gloom* written all over him. He began by having me make movements and testing me—my hearing, my heartbeat, and the sound of my lungs. I felt so good. He asked me some questions. I told him proudly about my mom having had breast cancer some forty-plus years ago and said that she was still doing very well. She would be eighty-six in December.

After just meeting this man for the first time, he asked Cindy and me if we wanted to hear his prognosis of my situation. We thought this was odd, as he hadn't really spent any time with me. How in the hell would he know anything? What did he know that my oncologist didn't? Where was this guy coming from?

Well, we agreed to hear him. He started to spoil our good moods rather quickly. Cindy and I were directed to sit across the room as he began his cold and negative prognosis. It began with, "Don't think that you're going to be like your mom." Next it was, "I wouldn't bother having a savings account," followed by the ignorant words, "What you have is *impossible to beat*." Cindy and I both knew that "with God, *nothing* is impossible." Dr. Gloom had missed that concept somewhere along the way, or he had just become so pessimistic at that point in his career, or . . .

I had about ten or so visits to receive the radiation to both my shoulder and my lower back. I was able to drive myself each and every time, and I did stop at the tackle store that was close by. Where Dr. Gloom was concerned, I was fortunate that I didn't have to see him on every visit. His staff took good care of me.

However, during my last visit, I had to meet with Dr. Gloom. I kept a positive attitude about my surviving all of this, just as Cindy and I had when we'd first walked into his gloomy office a few months earlier. He did tell me to stop by sometime in a couple of years and show him some big fish that I may have caught.

It's been well over four years and many fish later. I'll continue to drive by his office—on the freeway as I head to the lake—and I'll think, *Thank you, Dr. Gloom, for your service on my shoulder and back. And thank you for the extra incentive to prove you wrong. You simply fueled my tank of faith, hope, and optimism!*

Before my dear dad died of lung cancer, and before I was diagnosed with virtually the same thing, my mom would bring his dinner out to him at his work bench. He had his laptop set up on a little table with a pulley system on top of their dryer. He'd raise his computer operations when my mom needed to use the dryer. He had his Direct TV, stereo, radio, and a propane heater out there. He fixed many, many things in that garage, to so many people's delight. He was the best, with his "Yankee ingenuity" and his sign hanging above the work bench: "Popcorn Technology." He is our dad, Mario Ottavio Balanesi, an Italian marvel in our parts. My tears are welling in my eyes.

I Finally Had My Cry, and It Would Not Stop

I'm out here in my treasured garage as I write and putter around. It's an inherited thing, I guess: "like father, like son." It's my space. It's that creative place where you keep your stuff. My garage is where I keep my bass boat and all my tackle.

I installed a pretty nice stereo system on the boat some years ago. Skeptical friends said I'd scare away the fish. But I don't. I may play a particular music CD during take-off from the dock or when I am going through a five-mile-per-hour zone. The best part is having the sound and power to play the stereo out in the garage if I'm in the mood, and this was one of those moments.

Remember that I earlier mentioned the song "Just Gets Better with Time"? Well, that got me inspired to play the song on the boat. Since I was in sales and on the road all the time, I would listen to CDs and talk radio. When I was wooing Cindy back in '93, I had a Whispers CD playing. That was it. They had *exactly* what I wanted to hear, and to this day, there is nothing more romantic to me than to hear the music that brings me back to those early days of falling in love.

The Whispers were performing at the Empress Theater last year, which was just behind our new café location. Cindy put in a bid and got the job of feeding them and their production crew for their upcoming performance. It was unbelievably wonderful to have come into the café. (There go my tears again, as I feel such love for the honor of their time and appearance.)

The management of the Empress told Cindy, "No autographs, no photos." But when they came in, maybe they instantly felt God's presence and Cindy's warmth—that special ambiance. Before long, they were busy signing autographs and taking photos with genuine smiles and joy. (What's happening to me, God? I'm crying with love and appreciation for those talented guys.) They were so gracious to us that night. (I can't see through my reading glasses now. Can it get any better than this? Not without God and Jesus or humility and gratitude.) If you haven't heard "In the Mood" or "Just Gets Better with Time," you are missing out on the very best wooing music. It's timeless.

So, back to the story of having cancer return to my brain. I'm so excited about my life, what I have, who's in my life, all of it! My relationship with God and Jesus, my faith, and my love are so fantastic and unbelievable that I've been wanting to cry with joy. I usually don't cry, but I often get that knot in my throat while watching a movie or thinking of someone dear to my heart. My eyes will water with joy, appreciation, and love, but I can't seem to actually cry.

Well, after the song "Just Gets Better with Time" started, I began to bawl like I haven't done since I sat alone and asked God to spare my life and please forgive me for damaging my body. That cry had been good and was long overdue, but it was different from the cry I am having now.

My time out here in the garage, right now, is extra special, as it continues to rain tears. I'm thanking God for everything I have, including my opportunity to share this story with you. I also called Cindy at the café in order to share this wonderful experience with her. Wait until she gets home.

I needed this cry today. It's not about feeling sorry for myself or because of the cancer reoccurrence. On the contrary, it's simply my joy and the state of peace I'm feeling. The music just happens to really bring it on, and our experience with The Whispers that night was a godly thing. It wasn't a coincidence that The Whispers were performing that night. It was God's timing, His grace. Try Him. Don't wait like me to get cancer or have some other tragedy happen. Try God now. He's right here.

CHAPTER 6

Five Alarm, but First the Foot

The first of January 2007, Cindy closed the Good Day Café and headed around the corner to get gas. I was home in the midst of treatment, relaxing downstairs in my recliner. All of a sudden I heard the phone ring, and there was Cindy's voice calling out to me over the message recorder located upstairs: "Honey, honey, please pick up, pick up!" Her voice was in such high distress that I got up and did my best to get to the phone as fast as I could. She was trying to explain that an ambulance was arriving, that some lady had run over her foot at the gas station, and that she had to go to the emergency room at Kaiser.

Oh, my God! I got ready and drove over to the hospital where the ambulance was now heading with my poor wife. I couldn't get there fast enough. I went and found her somewhere in the back of the emergency area. She had already seen a doctor and had taken X-rays. There were no broken bones, just a shook-up wife with one shoe.

They gave her a support boot and some pain meds, and off we went. Some young lady driving through the gas station hadn't seen Cindy's foot and had driven right over it. And by the looks of things, it hurt. Cindy bravely used the support boot and went to the café the very next day. As she did, her foot healed quickly. Thank *Who*? Thank *God* for this!

What a start to 2007! And it got stranger. On Sunday, the seventh of January, Cindy had the day off. I often went to the café later in the day and after it had closed to pick up all of the receipts for deposit on Monday. Since I wasn't feeling up to it, we both stayed home. It's all relative what time you get up and what time you go to bed. We're usually in bed by seven or eight p.m., tops. We don't wait up to watch the evening news as we did in years past. We don't want to listen to or see negative news before we go to sleep. We want happy stuff. Give us comedies, please—even reruns. Then, before you know it, it's up and at 'em around three to five a.m.

Well, that night we were sawing the winter logs, when Cindy finally heard the message recorder located in the other room. She was awakened by the voice of Rose, her longtime, treasured employee, who is still with us today. She was anxiously trying to get hold of Cindy to tell her that the café was on fire.

Cindy got dressed as fast as she could. The cafe was on fire—a *big* fire, a *five-alarm* fire. I got up as well and had to follow Cindy after she rushed off in her car. By the time I arrived in my truck, the place had been cordoned off with fire trucks, police cars, and other emergency vehicles. A major fire was still burning the café and the motel rooms above it. We leased the café space and a portion of the parking lot from the franchised owners of the motel. No customers were inside or threatened at that point, and no one was hurt. Thank you, God. Thank you, Jesus, for your mercy! I found a place to park out of the way of the fire crew, but the smoke was way too strong for me to be looking around. I had never been in this type of environment before. My healing lungs could not take the smoke. (Here I go again with the tears, but these are not tears of joy.) It was an awful event. Camera crews were out from all the major Bay Area news stations and newspapers.

This was one of Vallejo's most popular restaurants, and for many, it was like their second home. Customers made their daily pilgrimages for their daily bread and their daily connection with other life forms. The place was known by many reporters who had covered a story or two in our city. It was a five-alarm fire, calling for help from neighboring cities. The Good Day Café was my wife's second home, her life's work, her passion.

Let me get to this now. Thanks to God, no one was hurt, even though people were staying in motel rooms above and right next door to the cafe. Thank you, God, for sending a local, off-duty police officer, a hero, our friend. He and his daughter happened to drive past the café, notice the fire in its early stages, and call 9-1-1. They also looked around for any injured people at the motel.

It was absolutely heartbreaking to see my wife under these circumstances—as if she didn't have enough going on. There were now seventeen or eighteen employees without jobs. It was a distressing burden on Cindy's shoulder—on top of my problems that she was already dealing with. Brave, and with so much community support, Cindy worked at putting the pieces of her employees' lives back together.

I was basically useless due to my situation. I did go looking for my wife's missing shoe from the weekend before. I don't remember if I was able to find it, now that I'm thinking about it. You talk about a man's ego? Mine was in the toilet because I couldn't help my wife. Cindy never came across in any way other than with love and the necessary strength to see this all through. She never made me feel that I was not there for her—not once!

One individual and two local groups held two special fundraising events for the café shortly after the fire. There had to be some closure on what had been a little oasis, a retreat, a daily getaway—like Cheers, if you would—where people knew your name and cared, a safe place to go and get some sunshine in the spirit and have a hearty meal.

My wife had created such a place, and as hard as a restaurant is to run, own, and manage, Cindy did one heck of a great job. Her personal slogan, printed on her menus and elsewhere, came directly from her heart to each and every customer: *We hope your dining experience will leave you feeling good in your tummy and in spirit.* In our very core, we had been sad to see many sweet seniors come and go because it was their time. How we would have liked to extend their time here on earth! They'll remain in our hearts and minds—and in many of photos and memories of having a "Good Day" with us!

There were many photographs taken of the fire and the restaurant crew. The community stepped right up for Cindy, and many came by the burned café to show their support and share hugs, kisses, and their sad regrets the following day. The outpouring was incredible.

Cindy's number-one concern was for her employees. A frequent and very popular customer immediately started to put together a fundraiser at the local Elks lodge. This was to include a spaghetti dinner with live entertainment and an auction. The date and time were set. Cindy's employees—and many others—all volunteered to help. It's still "tear time" for me, so I here I go . . .

The Community Opens Its Heart for the Café

The spaghetti dinner fundraiser was on. I drove over after Cindy had already left. I was still behind in everything, being in that chemo state of mind. I could at least drive and get myself around.

I need to mention here that neither Cindy nor I ever questioned God about this situation. We were already to the point where we both knew that something better was coming and that God was never to be blamed for this tragedy. It was in His master plan for us.

We remained strong in our faith and grew a stronger love for God. "No weapon formed against you shall prosper" (Isaiah 54:17). How's that for a comeback? Whatever lay ahead of us couldn't keep us down.

When I arrived at the Elks lodge, it hit me what my wife had lost—and gained. Here, more than 400 people who had bought tickets were arriving. I felt a little weird, as I still sported my chemo look, and I wasn't exactly a social butterfly, but this event wasn't about me anyway. Yes, the entire ordeal affected us, our family, and our lifestyle, as it was just before the housing market crunch, but this was about supporting my wife however I could. To see her stand bravely on the stage, to see and listen to the many people who loved her and had come out for the evening was incredibly wonderful and pulled on my tear chain. God and Jesus were with us, and with her, all the way through this. Something better was coming.

Believe, keep your faith strong, and don't give up or give in to the Devil. He'll get in your way, the closer you get to God. Watch out, and don't give in to him. He wants to get between you and God. He'll move on, and God will move you forward.

The activity that followed involved trying to get the show back on the road. Well, we soon learned that that wasn't going to happen, as the insurance agencies and fire department worked at finding fault for this two-million-dollar fire.

We talked with the landlord about coming back. He and his wife had already made up their minds that they would rebuild their own restaurant there. They had seen how good the business was, and they wanted it for themselves now. To them, we were bad luck, an accident waiting to happen again. So Cindy and I began looking all around the general area for a new site for the popular and successful café. I think we went and looked at about twenty places. Cindy was receiving insurance payments and had distributed the money received from the fundraiser to her employees as needed and had paid the necessary bills that came afterward.

After the event at the Elks lodge, the firefighters of Vallejo and the suburban Kiwanis planned another event. All of these wonderful people are givers. They give and give to their community with such enthusiasm and generous results. I am looking over their smiles and positive energy in the many photographs of the well-attended pancake breakfast they put on at the community center. A professional DJ from a popular Bay Area radio station was the MC. He is a special and dear friend of Cindy. I think that 740 people attended. This again gave testimony to just how popular the café had been and showed that Cindy was loved and appreciated by everyone. The entire crew of the café pitched in again to help serve and clean. These two events really demonstrated the incredible generosity behind those unselfish volunteer groups that serve our communities. As before, I didn't feel comfortable attending the event because of my chemo look and feel. I went to show my support to my wife and to give thanks to so many that helped.

Later on the morning of the pancake breakfast, one of our good customers called me outside and had a bunch of guys come and stand around me. They presented me with a jacket from their car club, "Boyz Under the Hood," and a plague with a model of a 1965 GTO—my first car and the one I most desire to have again. The club originally started in our now defunct café, and these guys were making me an honorary member. The jacket is so cool. They are a great group of guys and gals, now more than eighty members strong! Today they have their first-Saturday-of-the-month breakfast at the new café.

Cindy and I continued looking elsewhere to restart the café. We were very blessed to have been able to purchase a small home at a popular nearby lake—prior to the housing crisis and before I was diagnosed with cancer. We began looking up there for another café, to no avail.

But God had another plan. Cindy had had a small gift shop in the former café. She had really enjoyed having it, and she was now receiving signs from God to open a Christian gift store full-time. She prayed for answers, and they came. We went up to a small town at the other end of the lake and looked around for a place. She happened to ask one particular store owner about available spaces and learned that the very best spot on the street would be available soon. It was God's divine time, and He was directing us.

Cindy quickly talked with the husband and wife who owned the store and the building. These were really good people. (Here I go with those tears of joy wanting to come out in their honor.) He was a good man with a beautiful wife, and we appreciated both of them. We worked out a lease without all the red tape that we had endured with the former café. This was more person-to-person stuff. Yes, we did have a written agreement. Thank you, Jesus, for providing that place. It was the best location in town. It was located right on the corner with good visibility, good neighbors, and good landlords.

We went through a little upgrade and remodel, and soon Cindy had her store open. You could feel my wife's love in there. (Here I go again with those tears of joy.) I can still see her daily excitement, getting ready to go to her shop on time every morning. Cindy put in many hours every day. In the beginning, I was down there helping out too. (I was in remission and thought I was finally over this cancer stuff. I was wrong as you'll soon read.) We went to a furniture store and got what she needed for displays. We brought everything else up from our home and storage unit about 118 miles away.

I began having this nagging feeling behind my neck. It was a weird pressure. At times a kaleidoscope effect would appear around the edges of the TV screen, just moving around the perimeter. It only lasted a short time and then went away. As before, I asked around, and one person said that they saw the same effects, so I just forgot about it. But the slight pressure behind my head stayed and bugged me.

Cindy hired a handyman, so I didn't need to be at the store. I felt good otherwise, but I was never quite up to the job.

CHAPTER 7

The Cornucopia of Events That Are Still to Come

I guess that Cindy and her sister, who came up to help with the store, started to notice some changes coming over me. I still had that feeling of pressure behind my neck, and I just didn't feel really sharp. I couldn't help out at the new gift store. I soon learned that Cindy had no choice but to rat me out to my head nurse. That led to a call saying that I must see my oncologist immediately. Those finks.

I told you about the kaleidoscope effect that was happening around the TV screen. Well, on the morning that we were to go to the clinic, I drove my truck, and the girls drove right behind me, watching for anything unusual. As I was waiting for the girls so we could leave to go home, I looked at the headlight on my truck and saw that kaleidoscope effect around the headlamp. Go figure.

Now I had to act like nothing was happening. I didn't want to scare myself. So I went to God for His emergency help to get me safely off the hill and down to the freeway and home. The girls stayed right behind me. I was just hoping this wasn't a big deal.

You remember Dr. Gloom? He had said that a small cell in lung cancer will often work it's ugly way up to the brain. He had me take an open MRI, which was no more to my liking than a regular MRI. Dr. Gloom was probably disappointed, wanting me to come out positive. Well, that time, thanks to God, there had been no cancer noted—in spite of Dr. Gloom and the negativity I felt. Sorry!

We arrived for an MRI under my doctor's orders. I felt good at the time and was sure that everything was okay, but I learned that I had shingles. *What an awful name*, I thought, *for something on my body*. I had heard the word before, and it sounded so creepy. The nurse gave me something to take away my hatred of the MRI. It worked, and I felt more relaxed. Boy, oh, boy, has God blessed me with a great oncologist and team. (And here come those jerky, teary feelings. I've got to ask next week if chemo has a side effect that makes me tear up.)

We all returned to the lake house and store the following day. Cindy would receive the results from the oncologist soon.

And soon it was. My poor wife stood on the stairs outside so I couldn't hear. She learned that, yes, those tiny cancer cells were upstairs in my brain, and it didn't look good for me. My wife had to hear this from our trusted and now loved oncologist. This is hard to write, especially with this tearing-up activity that's happening to me, but I know that this surely will give me some credibility with you and with my Holy Spirit. I'm actually having the most special day. I can't remember when I had such pure peace and joy in my entire body.

Well, Cindy had her work cut out for her. She got me back down to our main house and set up caregivers for the time when I would be receiving radiation. She was there at the first meeting with the radiologist. This doctor was cool, and he was now accepting my insurance. The next good thing was that he was in the same building as my oncologist at the cancer center. My oncologist had me scheduled for some chemo sessions as a precaution in conjunction with the radiation.

Okay, we had a plan, but I never knew just how serious my condition was. Cindy knew but didn't tell me, because she knew I wouldn't want to know just how bad it really was. That was not part of my "war plan." I had to stay focused and keep my faith strong in beating this cancer thing. Now, how do you think I was getting through all of this? Through the love of my Holy Spirit and His constant presence, along with my faith. As promised, the Holy Spirit would always be there. Can you imagine having that combination, that supernatural power right there with you in your battle? There's no better combination!

The radiation soon took my hair out for the second time, and the radiologist said that it would come back different. Who knew? My caregivers all stayed overnight, and I truly enjoyed and greatly appreciated their services. Before I knew it, the experience was over. I took another MRI with a drug to relax me. The results all came back clear. I went back into remission.

Cindy and I realized that living at the lake with a gift store and paying mortgages on two homes with our much lower income would be difficult. Both of our homes quickly turned "upside down" with the downturn in the housing market. We were now the grandparents of two, and Cindy missed them and wanted to be closer to them. We were unable to rent out our main house in order to make the payments. Going between the two homes had become very tiresome and expensive. The only good thing about me being up at the lake house at such a distance from my oncologist was that the blood testing service was easily available and the air quality was so much better. In fact, it was the best air in the state.

However, in total agreement, we chose to move back to our main home and sell the gift store. We were going to get back into the restaurant business in the area where Cindy had her great reputation. We prayed and prayed. A year and a half after the fire, the old landlords called and requested a meeting. We briefly thought that this was by divine design. Coming back would get us going so much faster.

Then we slammed on the brakes. There was nothing enticing about going back to what had burned down and had been built back up without any—and I mean *any*—of Cindy's feedback. They had paid some outrageous price for an automated patio umbrella. This item alone demonstrated that the inside had been designed more for looks than for the functional needs of the day-to-day operation of the café.

The former landlord was now pleading, "Cindy, you are the only one who can make it here." But with the landlord's usual way of doing business and the cost of making the place operational, we decided the arrangement was not good for us. After three meetings, we were out of there fast. *Thank you, God!* We went on to look at another fifteen to twenty sites that were available in the general area for one kind of a restaurant or another.

In the meantime, I was getting over the shingles, and the oncologist had me stay in the hospital for a day or two because my body was now anemic. He put me into an isolated room while they treated me.

With that clearing up, we found a new place to locate the café, and we kept the same great name. We began the process of reopening almost two years from the date of the fire, but now, with the economy going the way it was, we didn't have the resources that we'd originally had when the cafe started in 1998, so it was a slower start out of the gate.

Still, we were moving forward. Since this book is not about financial aid, I'll spare you the details of our situation. Let's just say that the new Mercedes Cindy earned and owned outright was sold at a great loss, and I cashed in my declining 401(k), along with other assets.

You should now have a picture of two people who have kept their faith strong and stayed connected with God through the constant ordeals that could have taken them down. There's no way you will go down when you have the King of Kings, the Master of Masters, the Lord of Lords on your side. Are you getting a little excited? You may be wondering why God let you get into a particular mess on top of everything else in your life. It's all in His time and in His plans for us. As we learned, He's not giving us more than we can handle. Are we worthy of his great plans for us?

Cindy and I were both mature enough in our relationship with God to not let these things worry us or break our spirits—which is something the Devil will always try to do. The closer we get to God and Jesus, the more havoc and terrible means the Devil will use to keep us apart. You remember the truism: "Divided we fall, united we stand." The Devil wants you to try this all on your own, and he will cause more mayhem if you do. You see, this whole believing-in-God thing really works—if you work with God and Jesus. It's the only way. Doubt me? There is nothing bad about feeling at peace. Finally, for the past two years of my life, I have felt real peace. *Thank you, God! Thank you, Jesus!* Heck, the Devil's still trying to get us as I write these words.

While we were still looking for a place to reopen the café, a call came from a couple wanting to sell their restaurant. They learned that we were back in town and looking. We went to see the restaurant—reluctantly, since it was located in downtown Vallejo. That was an area we desired least, but Someone else liked it. Guess who had already been there a long time ago and knew we were coming?

We met with the owners and liked the inside dining and kitchen areas. Things were looking up. Speaking of looking up, I walked over to the transom windows above the left front door. As I looked up and out, I saw this bright light and felt the smile of God. He was confirming that this was where we should open, and we did. It was about the twenty-second place we looked at and prayed about. It came in His time: no sooner and no later.

There were various issues that needed to be worked out, but as it happened, Cindy was back in business almost two years from the date of the fire. The restaurant business is one of the most difficult businesses to operate successfully, and there we were, getting ready for a soft opening and then the Grand Reopening the following day. About nine days before those two events, we were to go through more of what I am being taught by God through this entire cancer thing.

I was down there at the new café every hour, helping to get ready, as I had done with the original café back in August of 1998. After feeling so good and helping out, I think I was drinking way too much coffee one morning and didn't stop soon enough to eat. I had finally sat down to eat a stale Danish, when suddenly I dropped onto the floor. I had a grand mal seizure and was biting my tongue. There I went, back to the hospital, where I stayed for two more days while my oncologist checked me out. Man, my tongue was sore. The seizure didn't last long, and it sure scared whoever was in the café helping us set up at that time. There were more tests, and that was it. The seizure has never returned since then. I do take a daily medication to this day.

My shingles were now gone. There's a light trace, a very light scarring on my skin that shows that they were there.

Smokers have no clue as to what they're subjecting their bodies to when they smoke. There are all of these side effects that go along with having stage four lung cancer. One morning I went downstairs to get our coffee going. I turned on the kitchen light, and all of a sudden a flash came to my right eye and would not go away. My oncologist referred me to an eye doctor. After being examined, the eye doctor told me that I'd had an eye stroke. This had happened behind the eye, so you couldn't see anything on the front of the eye. Now I see this little "cloud" in my vision as I look out, and it's so annoying. I see just fine when using both eyes—except for when I read. I have to use reading glasses for now, and the "cloud" is still here today, years later.

The next adventure came out of the blue more than two and a half years ago when a small blood clot appeared on my lung. The chemo began once again and my hair fell out for the third time. Cindy needed to give me two shots a day in my tummy (ouch) for fourteen days. And there were still a few more surprises to follow, tests from above.

In the meantime, the café was up and running. More and more old customers learned that Cindy had reopened. Every day, someone new found the café as well. It was a slower growing process this time, especially since the economy was so bad. We continued our prayers for our turnaround, our season. Our faith kept us strong and positive. It was coming . . . in His time. We knew that our Holy Spirit was with us. We continued to tithe ten percent of our income and saw the blessings that followed. If God was for us, who could be against us? (Romans 8:31)

Cindy and I needed to get her another car. The parents of our grandchildren needed a larger vehicle, and in today's economy, we needed to help them out. Cindy prayed for God's guidance, and we were led to the right car at the right dealer. After taking ownership, I had to take her car in for some service. The lady behind the service counter came out to give me an update as I was sitting in the waiting room. I had driven Cindy's car twenty-some miles to the dealership and felt great. But when the lady came out and it was my turn to talk, my words came out kind of spastic. I couldn't get control of what I was saying.

I was in the midst of having a TIA, a *transient ischemic attack*. They can last only a few moments or a couple of hours. Mine, fortunately, lasted for only a couple of seconds. Cindy happened to call just then and couldn't make sense of what I was saying. She headed over to the dealership while calling my nurse. The TIA was over pretty quick, and then I was in the truck with Cindy, heading to the clinic where the oncologist and nurses were waiting. They explained to us that this was a temporary interruption in blood flow to the brain.

This little event meant another overnight stay and yet another dreaded MRI the next morning. I asked and received the perfect relaxer, which made the MRI less horrible. I believe they gave me a good dose of Lorazepam. It seemed to do the trick, keeping me calm and making the MRI seem to end so much sooner. They actually had to postpone my MRI appointment due to a schedule conflict, so I received the relaxer prematurely. When the next scheduled MRI was ready a little while later, I had the same dose again.

As I described to others afterward, this particular MRI was like a Disneyland ride. I went down inside the unit, and there were these lit sconces on the walls. In my mind, it only lasted maybe five minutes and I was done. No sounds, no banging. Marvelous. I didn't feel all closed-in.

The results showed no problems, and I was later released from the hospital. The oncologist had me take an aspirin to thin my blood. It's been well over two years since the seizure and the TIA happened, with no reoccurrences. *Thank you, God and Jesus, for healing me and keeping me cancer-free.*

The café had its third-year anniversary on January 26, 2012. Therefore, it's been well over three years since that awful seizure. I continue to take an aspirin a day for the TIA and another med, as I mentioned, to prevent seizures.

The general checkups and biannual CAT scans would go on. Every month or two, I would go for a half-hour calcium drip to ensure that my bones stayed strong. I enjoyed the visits to the cancer center because they kept me humble, and I liked my nurses and the staff. They all played a role in keeping me going, year after year. A hug from my oncologist was good too!

My last CAT scan in 2010 got me a phone call while I was out on the lake, fishing in my boat. A voice said, "I am calling from the doctor's office. He told me to tell you that you're now in complete remission."

I said, "Can you say it again?"

Complete remission. I had never heard those two words put together at the same time. *Thank you, God and Jesus!*

CHAPTER 8

As I Walk (Again) through the Valley of the Shadow of Death

This is where it's going to get heavy. Are you ready? Are you believing? Let's go.

Psalm 23 was my turning point. I came across this particular Scripture when I returned to the valley of the shadow of death. My days of living under the impression of being in "complete remission" are over for now. The cancer is back, and I'm in the drip chair for more chemo.

This has shed more godly light on all of this than ever before. Revelation upon revelation has been revealed to me over a short period of time. Everything is in God's time. Have faith in Him and trust totally in Him, for He knows all and will reveal it when He is ready—and not a moment sooner. Once we can get this into our heads, we'll have the peace He promised us. It's a feeling He's been trying to give us all along, but we keep going our own way.

When I surrendered completely to Him, that feeling of true peace came over me with a comfort I'd never felt before. It feels good—even though our economy is still bad, world conflicts are terrible, and all this other stuff is going on. What a high—an incredible high. I want more of it! Even though I am back to "walk through the valley of the shadow of death, I will fear no evil."

I trust in God so much that my mind is open to receive all the pieces to my very own puzzle, and I thank Him all along the way. This puzzle was given to me at birth, but I didn't appreciate it. I didn't realize it was there, since I was so busy manufacturing my own pieces to the puzzle. I didn't even try fitting any of them together along the way. In fact, it was early this morning during prayer on my knees that I stopped and heard, "This is the rest of the story . . ."

All of a sudden a light came on inside my head. I was able to quickly and successfully put the rest of the pieces together. I immediately wrote this all down and sent it in an e-mail to my wife, as she was still asleep. I would read it to her later that morning while enjoying our coffee.

I told her that she had received an important e-mail and that I had printed it out for her. Of course she asked, "Who's it from?" and I said, "I forgot"—using this brain cancer thing to my advantage.

Below is that private e-mail. Before I start, though, I need to explain that my nickname for Cindy has been "Sweaty" for many years now. Not *Sweetie*. It's *Sweaty*—along with some variations. "Gross," you say. "Why?"

I call her by this name everywhere—yes, even in the café. I wrote a full-length screenplay years ago and had her proofread it. I used spell-check and apparently had misspelled *Sweetie* as *Sweaty* throughout—without the spell-check or me catching the error. The names I fondly call my wife are Sweaty or Sweat-alina—and then there's Sweaty-pie and Swa-tazo. This is like all the other junk in my mind; it's just a part of who I am. It doesn't feel right calling her Cindy anymore. So here is what I summed up that morning around two a.m. and later shared with my Sweaty-pie:

To my dear Sweaty,

I just prayed upstairs on my knees and was answered with this revelation:

Since God is anointing me, I still have lessons to learn. He has spoken to me through the only way that I would hear Him, and that's through cancer. But because of my strong faith in Him, He has called me and given me another exam, if you will.

He is bringing me back into "the valley of the shadow of death," and "I fear no evil, for Thou art with me."

He has now seen me "get" what was necessary to be anointed, to be a living testimony of His love and supreme powers. I know this to be a fact after my prayer this morning. I feel this revelation with every cell in my body. It all makes total sense to me now. After the last fifty-eight years, my life has come full circle. There's no doubt as to what I am destined to do for God and His Son, Jesus. This makes sense to me. Every bit of my life has been exposed and brought back together, piece by piece, by His mercy and His grace.

Thank you, my dear Sweaty, for being chosen as that one very special person here to lead me along, as hard as it was along the way.

"Do you love your wife?" you'll ask.

With all of my heart, I adore you!

Mr. B-Haven Himself

Coincidence is when God chooses to remain anonymous.

It's now the end of February, and my days of "complete remission" have been cut short. When I got the phone call that day on the boat while fishing, I was so happy to finally hear those two words connected. But the way I showed my excitement, my appreciation, my gratitude—mattered. I still didn't get it yet!

During my last CAT scan, taken in January of 2011, a spot or scar tissue was found on my brain. Everything below my neck was cancer-free, but there was a suspicious spot or spots (mets) on my brain. I did not say, "Why me, God?" or complain or feel down. I just knew that He was with me and was going to show me a missing piece to my life's puzzle that still needed to be exposed in order to put me all together. I hadn't quite been capable of understanding before, but God was determined and would not quit trying to tell me. He did so, loud and clear this time.

I'd been asking Him for so long, "What do you want me to do with my life?" But I didn't show Him the gratitude, as I should have, for Him and His Son and for what they had *already* given to me. Even Cindy recently mentioned my lack of appreciation for what I have. I had been stuck on what to do with myself, maybe feeling a bit sorry for myself, maybe being a tad depressed. But that didn't last long. I'm a slow learner, but when I do learn, I never forget, especially when it affects others.

My oncologist told me about this new spot he'd discovered on my brain and that I would also have to take an MRI to confirm it. He also mentioned chemo treatments as opposed to the risk of more radiation, which I'd had for the previous brain cancer.

Cindy always got the full scoop as to what I had and how bad it really was. I, on the other hand, didn't want to know all of the details. I am already dizzy just from writing this down. Too much information would only interfere with my battle plans. I could not lose focus on the mission at hand by dwelling on this or that. It has worked for me, keeping me out of the realm of Doctors Doom and Gloom's gloomy predictions.

The reality of having to go back and start taking chemo again hit me. There was the high possibility of losing my hair again. I had complained the last two times about how slowly it had returned, but I did like the simplicity and the fact that it had only a touch of gray. Lately I had been just getting by, feeling about ninety percent normal. I could still drive and looked forward to my fishing season arriving in a few more months.

But then this cancer thing came back. I have updated those who have been showing interest. I still have a positive mental attitude, but I don't have the peace or closure that I now feel I need. There is a 101-percent difference between who I was when I learned of this cancerous spot and who I am right at this moment.

God knew it was time to take me back into the valley of the shadow of death, and I knew it too. I hadn't yet received answers to my questions about what He wanted me to do, but I knew they would come in His time. I had overlooked many other little things, not appreciating them the way I do now. God knew, and I was instantly convicted by Scripture and by not wanting to be here in the valley for any longer than necessary. I mustered up enough strength and wisdom to realize where I was and how I'd gotten there.

Cindy had given me a laminated card with a picture of Jesus as a shepherd holding a lamb. He is shown helping a small flock of sheep through a doorway. On the other side of the card was Psalm 23. Cindy had added this card to greeting card for an occasion I do not remember. I carried this card with me and looked at it occasionally. Because it was laminated, it worked well on the dashboard of my truck, where I needed a business-card-sized object to hide an annoying light that came on from time to time. (No, it wasn't the check engine light.) The card worked perfectly, and I had that beautiful colored picture of

Jesus with me to look at and pray over anytime I drove. I would flip it around occasionally and read the reverse side.

The other recent time that Psalm 23 appeared was in a small daily devotional book that I keep in my fishing bathroom: *God's Little Devotional Book for Men*, published by Honor Books in 1996. It was funny how my sister-in-law helped get me that piece of in-home real estate, a third restroom downstairs, just off my garage. I got to decorate it myself with just fishing-related things. It ties into the fishing decor of my garage on the other side of the wall. I always read a short daily devotional before I picked up a fishing magazine. Inside this book was a reference to Psalm 23. Cindy gave me the book back in July 2001, and I've read it almost every day since then, so I came across this particular page from time to time. It started with, "Courage is resistance to fear, mastery of fear—not absence of fear." Then the page goes on to relate a short story that ties in to the introduction and Psalm 23. I just love this little book!

Earlier, I mentioned having a recent MRI in order for my oncologist to see how I was progressing with that spot in my brain. As it turned out, Cindy already knew that there were *several* spots. After only two chemo sessions that included six visits, this recent MRI showed a fifty-percent drop in the cancer activity already. The oncologist was pleased with these results, as was Cindy after seeing the oncologist.

I did not need to know that there were a number of these hot spots, but I know now. I just needed to keep myself moving forward with my thoughts focused on beating this new invasion. I knew that God was with me, and the number of warriors against me didn't matter. I was more concerned about the battle against this cancer and maintaining mind control, and less concerned with accounting issues such as the number of spots.

Regaining my driving privileges remains the second part of my goal during this next wait-and-see time. In the meantime, I take in stride all the other side effects from chemo—tiredness, diarrhea, and weird sleeping habits—with a full expectancy that life will get back to the top of the mountain in the very near future. Not a bad outcome for being such an ignorant guy for so many years.

I put it all together pretty quickly that God was taking me through this latest experience because there were more things He wanted me to reflect on and change. My changes had to be seen by Him, and those changes were just pouring out of me. I felt better and better with each new discovery.

Now, let's finish up on Psalm 23. There came a morning when one of our favorite pastors had his hour-long show on this particular Psalm. His sermon was excellent, meaningful, and sent by divine design. I was destined to turn on Dr. Stanley's show at that exact moment. I was fortunate to watch it several times that day. I saw, heard, and received God's message, as He desired.

The most important part of being where I am is to give thanks, as I am learning to appreciate my situation every moment. I have to figure that all of this was by divine design. I thank God for this experience. The chemo I could do without, but I believe it will be shorter than what the oncologist had planned. I believe that the spot will soon be gone, and I'll be up and out of the valley as a much better person. I believe that this experience is my turning point. The upcoming MRI will tell, and then I'll tell you!

With these new chemo sessions planned and now part of my weekly activity, I suspect I will be losing my hair again. I read a particular journal entry of the national lung cancer group that I joined back in 2008. This site, www.Inspire.com, has been an excellent opportunity to not only share my experience having cancer but to correspond with people all over the country who may be fighting lung cancer. This has given me the stepping stones I needed to give hope and, most importantly, to share my experiences and the successes that God has graciously given me. My faith has grown stronger and stronger, and my communications on this site may have touched people who needed positive material like the things I love to share.

Here's one of my last journal entries, inspired by another member who wrote about chemo's hated and often most-dreaded side effect, losing your hair. I wrote:

"Hair Loss: Another View" (written and posted February 24, 2011 at 2:45 a.m.)

I have had the greatest revelation regarding my own hair, one that I hope will help someone through a difficult possible result of this cancer thing we share. Just the other night as I was writing, I happened to grab my hair, and to my surprise, it was coming out. I am back in the chemo chair for a short time and had hoped that my hair wouldn't fall out again. I was out in my garage, typing, while Cindy and her sister went for their power walk. I just happened to reach up and grab onto my hair and noticed that I was able to pull it out.

Before I could get control of what was happening, God spoke to me faster than a Don Rickles comeback: "Now you can say you lost it for the fourth time!"

It gets better. I immediately went upstairs, excited, and shaved it all off. I had done nothing before but complain about how my hair grew back the second and third times. I didn't appreciate what God had given me, so after I had cleaned myself up, my dear wife commented on how good I looked, and I agreed. I was feeling so good about this new Marine Corps look.

I woke up early the next morning, still loving it and *very* grateful that I was still here. I promised Jesus that I would forever keep it that way in honor of Him and His Father to show my love and appreciation to Them. I went on to thank Him for letting me keep my moustache and goatee.

When my wife came downstairs that following morning, I told her what I wanted to do and asked what she thought. She supported me 101 percent. Mind you, since this cancer thing happened over five years ago, I am not the same guy. I have the Holy Spirit living inside of me, and I have a whole new outlook and life ahead. I am so blessed and grateful.

Next, another big thing happened, and this is the truth. Cindy's dad had done something similar, and she had wanted to talk to me about it but wasn't sure if she should. She told me that she had gone to her dad's house before he passed. He came to the door with a shaved head. A very handsome man, regardless, he had asked his daughter, "How do you like it?" She had answered, "It looks good," and then asked him, "Why?"

His reply was that he spent way too much time on his vanity and not enough time with God! This new look, for me, will be an outward sign of my love for Jesus and His Father, who are the only ones that could have made this at all possible. My shaved head is a sign of *hope* for those who have cancer and are still fighting the battle.

CHAPTER 9

After All of This and That

Thank you so very much for reading my book. Now that you've nearly finished, I hope that you have gained, been inspired, or learned something—no matter how small or trivial it is—about dealing with these things that life and the Devil throw at us. The free will that we are born with, coupled with being sin-free—thanks to the sacrifice of Jesus Christ, who died on the cross for our sins—has started us out with a clean slate. And look at what many of us have done to mess it up.

If you're not in a relationship with God and His Son, Jesus, I hope that you will begin to develop one. We most highly recommend this as a starting point in living a more fulfilled and peaceful life. As soon as you begin your walk with these living Spirits and accept them as real, as the most important part of your life, you will start feeling better, happier, and healthier.

I've given you the truth. Cindy and I are living proof of God's love, proof that He and Jesus hear prayers. The question always remains: are we listening to Them and following God's Word? Until I was diagnosed with cancer, I would never think to actually enjoy sitting and reading the Bible. Now I do.

Life itself is now most important to me, which was something I'd never realized before. It's no longer about the money, what I have acquired, or what I still want. It's now about having a peaceful life—wanting less and tithing more, sharing more, giving back more. In other words, I want to spend the rest of my life giving back so much more. The first half was always about taking and wanting more and more and giving barely anything back.

At the end of this book, I have recommended some materials to help and encourage you when you or someone you love is faced with cancer or some other tragedy. One of my closest and dearest friends just told me that he had never heard me being down or having a negative attitude about what Cindy and I were going through. I guess it's true that we are being observed by others. We desire only to set a godly example.

Let me update you now before I sign off. My latest MRI results came back showing that the cancer in my brain has now shrunk because of the treatment and care of my oncologist. I am in remission again. My big question was, can I begin to drive? The answer was no. An EEG and a visit with a referred neurologist supported my oncologist's answer to my question.

With that said, I am now on another adventure, a life of not driving—other than driving my wife crazy. I have driven almost half a million miles, doing my job as a sales rep along with all my other driving over many years. That has now ended. At first I was upset, but Cindy quickly reminded me that I was in remission.

My oncologist was truly saddened that he had to tell me this bad news. He went on to say that he wanted me to take additional chemo as a preventive measure to keep me clean and clear of a reoccurrence. I soon got over my whining and agreed with what he desired for my well-being. I know that when one door is closed, God promises to open another door! I have faith that this ruling will be reversed someday, but I am not going to tie myself up with any further whining. I am looking forward to the good that will come from this new fact that I can no longer drive. I am alive!

To date, I have been fishing seven times in my boat in 2011 and once already in 2012, because my buddy and my brother have eagerly helped get me and my bass boat to the lake and river for days of fishing bliss! It got to the point where we were able to stay out on the river for eleven hours straight. I had trouble getting around the boat, since chemo affects my balance a bit. But the fifth time I was on my boat and having a hard time getting around, I began using my stoutest fishing rod to hold myself steady as I moved about. This gave me the idea of finding a rod or staff, as I remembered that Cindy had stocked them at her Christian gift store.

I now meet one of my friends at our café for breakfast once a week. That friend will kindly drive me to the next city in order to get my blood test. Friends trade off and help me get to the clinic, since Cindy has to stay at the café. One particular time, I asked Judi if she could bring me to an ACE hardware store after the blood draw so I could pick up a new hacksaw blade. I quickly looked around, and there, of all things, were staffs in a variety of lengths. I found the perfect one and use it to this day.

There are many times when I wish I could drive with my oncologist's blessing. Specifically, I wish I could help my wife by running errands for the café. But I can't, so I have to be extra creative and do what I can here at home to help her out. Now that I have the Holy Spirit active in my heart and soul, I can look forward to what God has planned for me.

I hope I can inspire someone with my stories of what made it possible for me to carry on. Remember Hawkeye on the TV series M*A*S*H and his "carry over, Cary Grant, cash and carry, hari-kari, carry a tune, carry on, carry out, carry over . . ."? Goofy little things like this are releases of my sense of humor over the negative thoughts that come out and try to overshadow my faith and belief that I will win this fight with cancer. These simple things have driven Cindy nuts, but they have helped (here we go again) "carry" me through it all. A friend and former customer who is fighting cancer sent this quotation in her update:

> Life is not about surviving the storm.
> It's about learning to dance in the rain."

Cindy and I tithe ten percent of our income monthly. It's not a big deal. Your mind may play tricks on you and give you a negative feeling about tithing. You might think you can't afford to give God ten percent of your gross earnings, or you won't be able to pay for this or that. However, you'll always make it, because God knows the spirit by which you tithe.

The most important element of my life is my growing relationship with God and Jesus. One aspect that has become extremely valuable is watching spiritual programs on TV and backing off the junk! Many pastors and ministers are truly inspirational, and sometimes their sermons have been exactly what we needed to hear that specific day, time, and hour. Remember what I said about my "walk through the valley of the shadow of death" and how Dr. Stanley happened to have a show on that particular Psalm. That didn't just happen; it was by divine design, period.

Another most excellent resource is the collection of daily devotionals I receive on my computer from Joel Osteen Ministries. Lately, it's like God is talking through Joel to Cindy and me. I make copies and share them with Cindy, as she'll share her readings from Joyce Meyer's *Starting Your Day Right* for each morning of the year and *Ending Your Day Right* for every evening of the year—two books in one. Cindy will also share something from her favorite study Bible by Dr. Stanley, the *Life Principles Study Bible*. I also have a dear friend Kim, who will kindly forward several other devotionals to me.

Please believe me. If you don't give these resources a try, it's going to be harder to make it. I have to be blunt. If a person I am corresponding with doesn't have a relationship with God and definitely has no desire for one, it's much harder to communicate with this person, and he or she may very well lose his battles. Having certain Scriptures drilled into your brain through God's help and His divinely designed interventions will help you remember things like this: "If God is for us, who can be against us?" *No one!*

Having this kind of spiritual food constantly going into your body will help you beat whatever is coming against you, your family, or your friends. Cancer is a *very* formidable enemy! You'll need God and His Son to help you! Remember that every medicine, every method, and every tool used by our doctors, medical teams, and scientist are gifts from God only. He has blessed those who develop and use such resources. Man is nothing without God's intervention.

Just one more thought before I close. Another example of God's divine design involves some special new friends that Cindy met at the café and recently introduced me to. This couple have become regulars at the café. During one of their visits, Cindy learned that the husband, Dave, had recently been diagnosed with both brain and lung cancer. *Bingo.*

Cindy took responsibility for getting him and me together shortly afterward. We met at the café one day, along with his loving wife, Misty, and their wonderful son and beautiful daughter. We hit it off immediately, especially as we are brothers in this fight against cancer. They are a Christian family and are acquiring more weapons needed to fight this battle together. We have lots to talk about almost daily. He was diagnosed back in June of 2011. I knew immediately that Dave was properly armed with God as his commander in chief, and he had incredible support from his family and friends.

I hope that some of my experiences will help Dave and his family get through this terrible battle. He has sure been great to talk to about our similarities. His friendship, along with daily correspondence, has been a blessing to me from God. Our lives have changed forever. I won't be going back to the life I once had, as I have already begun this new chapter.

I talked with Dave just this morning, and I remembered to tell him that I'm not so crazy after all. There happen to be—as I read and saw in a recent report on Fox News—giant rats that sniff out tuberculosis. He went on to tell me that he had read about dogs that can smell lung cancer. CAT Scans, PET Scans . . . hmm . . . not so crazy after all. He calls them the "Animal Scans." I wish that I could take credit for that term!

I'd like to think that it's over, but it's not. I have been in the chemo chair every three weeks for many months now. My oncologist says that it's "maintenance" in order to keep the brain cancer at bay. Is there more for me to learn? There's *always* more for me to learn as I strengthen my faith and resolve to beat this.

I have taken another EEG recently, and my brain seems to remain uninterrupted with signs of any seizure activity. That's good, but there remains a spot on my brain that is a concern. Another recent MRI showed a small spot that the radiologist said was cancer. My oncologist told Cindy and me that he didn't think it was. As we looked at the spot, it was unclear, looking almost as though it was being erased. Something like this had happened before. My oncologist had tried to show Cindy something, but when he went to find it, whatever it was had disappeared. Doubt me?

I want to add another story that a new friend inspired me to share. I met this friend on the "Inspire" website for people who look for information, friendship, and like minds in similar situations. I hadn't posted anything for a while, and this new friend was just following up on me and my progress. I had been thinking of writing the following account as a journal entry. The original version did not get posted on Inspire but was instead lost in a black hole. This rewritten version offers a new approach to sharing, encouraging, and giving back. Thank you Liz, of Liz and Berry.

As I go to receive my treatments about every three weeks, I now request one of the two community rooms in the back of the oncology department, as opposed to taking a private room. One of the nursing assistants takes my vitals up in the front area and then kindly escorts me to where the nurses are prepared for my two-hour drip. As we walk back to the nurses' station, we pass by a number of private rooms. The assistant will offer me one of those rooms, which I previously preferred. But I now thank them and request that I be seated in the community room without the TV, where there are reclining chairs and machines to administer the bags of chemo. I figure, why take a private room when it is such a welcome site to most people for comfort and privacy? Each has its own TV and is very comfortable. I, on the other hand, who once cherished the private room, pray that I will have the privilege and honor of meeting someone who may need or like my company. Maybe someone can use some hope, inspiration, or just a smile.

Each time, my prayer is answered, and someone comes into the community room who lifts my spirits, as I hope I have done for theirs. One time, I was almost through my drip. I had been reading and talking to one of the friendly nurses that was assigned to treat me that morning. A lady walked in, followed shortly by her husband, who was the one to be treated. I said hello to them, and we began to talk. I thanked God for this opportunity. It wasn't much more than just a chance to listen and share. Thinking of my own wife, it touched my heart to see this loving couple working together. I wouldn't have had those special moments had I said yes to a private room—and that is the whole point.

Another man who came into that room midway through my session was surrounded by his wife and family members. I could see that he needed help to sit in the chemo chair. He had been rolled into the room on a special bed. The family was speaking Korean, and one of the nurses spoke their language and was able to help the older man with his treatment.

While he received whatever was dripping into his body, we would sometimes make eye contact and transfer a warm smile to one another. As we both seemed to be finished, help arrived to assist the older man onto a carrier that took him out of the oncology department. His smile had touched my soul, and as I walked by him, we smiled again, and I was able to reach out and actually touch him. It was my way of saying, "You have touched me, sir, and that was my love pat back to you."

Do you think that I'd change these little experiences and go back to watching the news in a private room? No way! This is what healing is also about. It is very powerful and a sign that Jesus is with us. I just saw that Korean man sitting comfortably in his own private room the other day. As I walked by, I stopped in his room. He smiled, and his wife sat up to greet me as well. We shook hands and felt that special bond.

The last person I met in the community room happened to be a pastor. He was such a handsome and well-spoken man. Cindy happened to be with me during this special visit, because we had to see my oncologist that afternoon. I was to have some blood drawn by one of the nurses so that I could be tested for a new trial drug that my oncologist wanted me to try as opposed to more chemo. Again, I had requested the community room. The pastor that we enjoyed meeting came to our café the next day, and Cindy was able to welcome him. We'll pray and wish him God's miraculous healing powers. This pastor named, Anthony, knows the true benefit of prayer and just how important it is to have God and His Son in your life as you battle this beast called cancer.

So now it was back to that MRI (Miserably Rude Instrument) for another look-see. I knew that my Holy Spirit would be with me. Cindy and I have put this new situation in God's hands and keep our faith strong and prepared for whatever comes.

I feel good, and there is no sign that the cancer is somehow interfering with my day-to-day activities. I believe that all of the chemo I have received over the years—and am currently receiving—has made me a little off-balance. Hence the staff that I now have on my fishing boat. In no way do I have the stamina that I once had. But heck, I was able to stay out all day on the Delta for eleven hours!

As I prepared myself for the outcome of the next MRI, I thanked God for healing me and that I was here to share this. The results came back, showing that the spot was still there. Cindy and I went for a consultation with the radiologist next door. I continued to receive chemo while another consultation was arranged up in Sacramento for a "gamma knife" radioactive procedure. Am I scared? No, because I have God with me and I am here to stay.

Thank you for your time in reading this. May God bless you and everyone who has stayed with us through our story.

Dear Jesus,

I hope that this little book will have helped one or more readers get in contact with You and Your Father. Your lines are never busy and are always open, twenty-four seven. Now Cindy and I both know how to do this thing called life in a way we never before imagined—with joy in our hearts and a true peace in our souls.

This is the truth, and, as the saying goes, with my left hand raised and my right hand on my Bible in front of Cindy, I say, "So help me God!"

Humbly yours,
Jim Balanesi

Resources

The following is a partial listing of all of our favorites, and there are so many, many more.

Resource #1 is a must-read: the Holy Bible. Cindy uses Dr. Charles Stanley's *Life Principles Study Bible*, and I read *The Men's Devotional Bible, NIV*.

TBN (Trinity Broadcast Network)
PO Box A
Santa Ana, CA 92711-2101 www.TBN.org

CBN (Christian Broadcast Network)

Angel One

DayStar TV Network

It's Not About the Bike: My Journey Back to Life by Lance Armstrong is truly an inspirational book of courage and victory. In 1997 he founded the Lance Armstrong Foundation which supports people affected by cancer. This was one of the first books I read, which my older brother had recommended.

Knockout: Interviews with Doctors Who Are Curing Cancer by Suzanne Somers is a great resource, and she is a super inspiration, as she includes her own personal battle!

Lifechurch.tv is a website that was recommended to me by my new brother in battle Dave. I really, really like this site and what they offer. I can easily turn on the sermons whenever I want. Thank you, Dave!

Inspire.com is an excellent website helping people with lung cancer. It's both educational and supportive, and you'll meet many people who have gone or are going through what you are.

Noreen Fraser is the author of *Staring Down Cancer* and cofounder of Stand Up to Cancer, featured on FOXNews.com. These articles that she has published are often available on FOXNews, and they are very inspirational and informative to read. Thank you, Noreen, for sharing your fight as well as fighting for others by raising money through your foundation.

LUNGevity.org: I only very recently came across this "pot of gold" while searching through FOXNews.com. I have only begun to look into this advocacy organization that was established to generously raise money for research and public and political awareness of this too-common killer, lung cancer.

Ministries and Pastors

Pastor Charles Stanley, In-Touch Ministries
PO Box 7900
Atlanta, GA 30357-9979

"In Touch" is an excellent weekly show and such an inspiration. We love this man!

Joyce Meyer Ministries
PO Box 655
Fenton, MO, 63026 joycemeyer.org

"Enjoying Everyday Life" is a weekly show and an excellent source of food for the soul. Joyce is an author of over eighty books! She and her husband, Dave, are a wonderful inspiration!

Joel Osteen Ministries
PO Box 4271
Houston, TX 77210 joelosteen.com

TV show: *Joel Osteen*
Joel and his wife, Victoria, send out their daily devotional, "Today's Word," via e-mail. It is inspirational and very valuable to share with others and to save to read again and again.

Kerry Shook Ministries
PO Box 131444
The Woodlands, TX 77393
1-866-226-9866 kerryshook.org

This has become Cindy's favorite "go-to" show shortly after she gets up at four a.m. I enjoy it as well. It's excellent!

John Hagee Ministries jhm.org
We enjoy these powerful, weekly, father-and-son sermons of John Hagee and his son Matthew.

The 700 Club with Pat Robertson and his son Gordon is a daily show with excellent resources for inspiration, prayer, and world news (cbn.com).

It just cracks me up when valued shows like the ones mentioned above pay for airtime with one of the major networks, and an adviser's voice comes on the air to say something like: "The views and opinions expressed by the following show are not those of . . ."

It happens to be the best stuff on the network!